GOOGLE APPLICATIONS

For 21st Century Educators & Learners

Dr. Maneesh Kumar Bajpai

Dr. Preeti Sharda

Ess Ess Publications

New Delhi

GOOGLE APPLICATIONS
For
21st Century Educators & Learners

ISBN : 978-81-947398-1-4

Price : Rs. 600/-

First Published 2021

Published by:
Ess Ess Publications
4831/24, Ansari Road,
Darya Ganj,
New Delhi-110 002.
INDIA
Phones: 23260807, 41563444
Fax: 41563334
E-mail: info@essessreference.com
www.essessreference.com

Cover Design by *Patch Creative Unit*

Printed and bound in India

Contents

Preface

The technology is giving solutions to the problems encountered during the normal conditions or any abnormal condition like COVID pandemic 2019-20. Lockdown was imposed to save the people from the virus which immensely affected the diverse field of education, business, and development. Education is a very important aspect in the growth of society and the preservation of the culture. The physical classroom teaching and interaction is not possible yet. The library and resources are not accessible physically for teaching and learning. So, everything was affected from March 2020 in India.

Information communication technology came into the picture which gave an opportunity to everyone in the field of education and others to appreciate teaching and learning. Online videoconferencing tools, digital libraries, and electronic resource management software, etc helped in the dissemination of the information and contents to the students, faculty members, and research scholars in urban and rural part of the country. Even, globally, anyone may be reached over the internet for enhancing and continuing the research and education or other purposes too. Several educational and awareness programmes were organized during the pandemic period over the webinars platforms to educate and impart education.

During several interactions with the students and research scholars and teachers of rural areas, we understood that they are not aware of the platforms which are useful for them or the cost is a great concern. How to access and how to download and how to use for their research and study was some questions were raised during the conversation with many students and research scholars. Keeping in mind the requirement of such students and faculty members, we started working on this project. The idea behind *'GOOGLE APPLICATIONS For 21st Century Educators & Learners'* is to give solutions to the students. Google is one of the popular brands which is known for various applications which are useful for research and study purposes. It is useful for the students and teachers both as communication and teaching and learning. It is a boon for the libraries in disseminating digital resources and services to their students. The volume is spread into ten chapters which fully expressed Google applications.

Google Classroom is one of the best of its class in the dissemination of study materials, maintaining attendance, and grading the performance of the students. Students, teachers, and librarians may coordinate to extend the teaching and learning activities. Even, the quiz may be taken too to revise the syllabus and all. Blogging and site are very useful for libraries to reach to their users with innovative library services and resources. YouTube may be one of the applications which may be used by the teachers to create their channels and reach the students by the recorded lectures. Google meet is available for real-time teaching and interaction purposes. All these are available free of cost at the rate of internet cost or data packages to everyone. We have tried to shape the volume in a more practical method which may be used by the students, research scholars, librarians, and teachers to empower the education through google applications from anywhere anytime round the clock.

(Dr.) Maneesh Kumar Bajpai

(Dr.) Preeti Sharda

राजा राममोहन राय पुस्तकालय प्रतिष्ठान
RAJA RAMMOHUN ROY LIBRARY FOUNDATION
संस्कृति मंत्रालय, भारत सरकार
Ministry of Culture, Government of India
Block-DD-34, Sector-1, Salt Lake City, Kolkata-700 064
Phone : 2337-3463/64/65(FAX) | Web : rrrlf.gov.in | E-mail : rrrlf-wb@nic.in

F.No. 3-2/DIR/DCOR/2021-22 Date: 22.05.2021

FOREWORD

My immense pleasure urges me to proclaim that Dr. Maneesh Kumar Bajpai, Deputy Librarian &Head-Madhu Limaye Library, Dr. Ram Manohar Lohiya National Law University, Lucknow, and Dr. Preeti Sharda, Librarian, Post Graduate Government College for Girls-42, Chandigarhhave penned a book entitled 'Google Applications For 21stCentury Educators & Learners', which elucidates the usefulness of the most deserved web applications among the intellegentia.

Now a days, the rampant curse of COVID-19 has emerged as a global pandemic that has spread over 215 countries worldwide and disrupted various industries around the world. However, every dark cloud has a silver lining. It has taught each one of us to adapt and transform ourselves towards digital environment based on computer and communication technology, which are the prime sources of connecting each other towards imparting education-teaching & learning, dissemination of information and its resources. The incompetencies and amateurishness on updated technologies is the major obstacles in the exchange of knowledge and information between information seekers and information providers. Google applications, which, being widely used and popular among academia, are one of the best possible options to bridge between those information seekers and information providers to allay the thirst of information. The book encompasses all basic and useful applications viz. chrome, meet, classroom, sheet, google site, youtube etc., which are aptly useful in each level of the learning pyramid. It will work like a handbook for teachers, students and library science professionals in exchanging the domain of knowledge and information.

I applaud the authors once again for their commendable work.

With Best regards,

Ajay P. Singh 22/05/21
Prof. (Dr.) A. P. Singh

1

The GOOGLE

Its Applications and Extensions

Google came into existence in 1995 at Stanford University. Larry Page and Sergey Brin, two students of the university while working on a research project, built a search engine "Backrub" with a mission 'to organize the world's information and make it universally accessible and useful'. The search engine used links to determine the importance of individual pages on the World Wide Web. Soon the search engine got a new name Google (phew). The project went well and found investors for it and in August 1998, Sun co-founder Andy Bechtolsheim wrote invested $100,000, and thus Google Inc. was officially born. In 2015, it named itself as 'Alphabet' bringing together all the Google products and services under one umbrella. Today Google is the third-largest company in the world. Today Google is in everything, it has Web-based products which include Search tools, Advertising services, and Communication and publishing tools; it has Development tools which include Security tools, Map-related products, and Statistical tools; it is into the development of Operating systems, Desktop applications, and Mobile applications also. Recently it has also entered into the market of Hardware production.

PRODUCTS AND SERVICES OF GOOGLE FOR EDUCATION

Google has developed many products and services. These products are very easy to deploy, use, and manage and can be used anytime, anywhere, on any device. Google has categorized its products and services as 'Watch & play', 'Devices made by Google', 'Use anywhere', 'Talk &text', 'Stay organized', 'Work smarter', and 'Grow your business'. Google has developed many products, programs, and philanthropy to help the educational institution and to improve the teaching-learning process. In the following section, Google Chrome and Google apps for education are discussed in detail, which can make the teaching-learning process very smart, efficient, and flawless.

GOOGLE CHROME

Google Chrome is a free cross-platform web browser and was launched by Google in 2008. All Google services work better with Google Chrome. It is more than just a web browser. It manages its system resources differently than other browsers. Essentially it is an operating system that functions on the cloud. It helps in synchronization of all the Google services and Google accounts, it enables tabbed browsing, and helps in automatic translation and spell check of web pages. Chrome is configured in such a way that its updates are downloaded automatically. Chrome is a very fast and reliable browser that has numerous built-in and add-on benefits. To make maximum use of Google Chrome user has to sign in with Gmail account. It will help the user to save and sync bookmarks, history, passwords, and other settings to his Google Account. Even if he uses another device to use chrome he will get similar settings. Slight changes in Google Chrome can make it more usable and user friendly.

GOOGLE APPS

Google Applications or Google Apps are "a suite of web-based messaging and collaboration applications that Google hosts on their servers" (My Apps Georgia Southern University Learning Center, 2020). These are services, not software. Anyone can easily use these apps through the web browser only, no need to download them as we do with other applications and software. The biggest benefit of using Google apps is they can be installed quickly even without restarting the computer or browser. For using these apps one has to sign in so they can be sync across multiple computers. We don't have to update them and they never crash the computer as they are hosted on the web and nothing is saved on the computer. These apps are very easy to use and very easy to search and one can open the app using app launcher. All the programs have web, mobile and desktop versions. Main benefits of using Google apps-

1. Almost every application is free to use and safe as Google is involved.
2. Nothing has to be downloaded every app can be accessed through the web browser.
3. Everything is saved in Google drive (eventually on Google servers), so the space problem is solved and data can be accessed anywhere and anytime using any device.
4. Real-time collaboration and file sharing is possible;
5. Automatic updation by Google only.
6. User doesn't have to create a different username password for every app, every app can be accessed through Gmail username and password.

There are two types of Google Apps firstly "Apps which work as regular websites like Gmail or Calendar" and "Apps that work like software programs in the desktop, relying on certain features of Chrome, like, Google Keep". In the following section working of all the Google apps is being briefly discussed. Categorization of the apps is also done according to the purpose for which they can be used.

OFFICIAL DOCUMENTS PREPARATION

Google has many applications but it has three applications that are specifically made for Office Management. Google Document (docs), Google Spreadsheets (sheets), and Google Presentations (slides) are the Web-based applications to create official documents provided by Google to create, edit, share, and print documents. Many templates are made available. Real-time collaboration is possible using any device. Whatever is done in these documents is automatically saved in Google Drive. Google doc is "an online word processor to create and format text documents"; Google sheet is "an online spreadsheet application to create and format spreadsheets and charts"; and Google slide is "an online presentations editor to create visual presentations and shows".

Google Docs : Google Docs is an online word processor to create and format documents and work with other people. "It is a cloud-based document solution with real-time collaboration and powerful tools to compose, edit, and share documents". It has ready-made templates for writing Resumes, Letters, Personal, Work, Sales, Legal, Human Resources, Freelance Management, and Education which can be used while creating a document.

Google Sheets : Google Sheets or a worksheet is a file made in a tabular format consisting of rows and columns, for visualizing, calculating, and organizing the data. It is a free, web-based spreadsheet program provided by Google since 2014 and it is almost similar to the Microsoft Excel programme. Google Sheets is a convenient method for real-time collaboration, compilation, sharing, reviewing, and presentation of data and information. It can do complex analysis and can handle 2 million data sets. It is very easy to use and various readymade templates are available and supports about 83 languages. The major benefit of using Google Sheets is one can edit and share their spreadsheet files over the internet making them useful for all kinds of works. Many third-party add-ons enhance the usability and functionality of Google Spreadsheets. Google sheet gives the facility to create their dashboards; write formulas use of built-in applications to automate any job.

Google Slides : Google Slides is a web-based free presentation programme provided by Google since 2006, which can be used to create, edit, and collaborate with others to make professional presentations and present wherever you are. Google Slides is an incredibly versatile tool. Google slide is powerful presentation software and it's very user-friendly. It's Google's equivalent to Microsoft PowerPoint or Apple's Keynote. Many features have been added over the past few years and Google is continuously updating it.

STORAGE

A Google account holder gets 15 GB of free storage, which is shared by Google Drive, Google Photos, and Gmail, which can be upgraded to 100 GB.

Google Drive : Google Drive is a cloud storage and backup service provided by Google since 2012. This service allows a user to save files stored as documents and photos from any of his devices including his smartphone, PC, laptop, or tablet. Google is very simple to use and is very well organized via drive. Retrieving the data from the drive is very easy.

Google Photos : Google Photos is a photo and video syncing service provided by Google since 2015. A user can store photos up to 16 megapixels and videos up to 1080p resolution. The service automatically analyzes photos, identifying various visual features and subjects. Users can search for anything in photos, with the service returning results from three major categories: People, Places, and Things.

COMMUNICATION

Google has made conversation and communication very easy with the following apps :

Gmail : Google Mail is a free emailing service, which was fully launched by google on 7 July 2009. It is very secure, simple, and easy to use, and it can be accessed through devices like PC, laptops, smartphones, or tablets. Customizable tabs like Primary, Social, Promotion, Updates, Forums are available in the email inbox which automatically segregates the emails. A Gmail user can organize all the emails received in various folders, to retrieve them easily. Gmail also provides the facility to view the attachments, RSVP to events, snooze messages and more without opening any email. Gmail is very secure as Google says that it blocks 99.9% of dangerous emails.

Google Groups : Google launched Google Groups in February to create discussion groups for people sharing common interests. This service helps to create and participate in online forums and email-based groups for conversations and discussions. It helps to send a single email to everyone in the group. There are four types of Google Groups namely 'Email List', 'Web Forum', 'Q & A Forum', and 'Collaborative Inbox'. Google Groups helps the participants to collaborate and share documents with a group.

Contacts : Google Contacts is the heart of Google Services and an online address book. It is the 'Contact Management Tool' and a standalone service that is freely available to Gmail users. Google Contacts can be used to keep track of email addresses, phone numbers, or physical addresses. It's probably not something you open often or even know exists, but it's worth checking out if you're a Google user. These can also be used to create Google groups.

Google Form : Google Form is a survey administration software provided by Google since 2014 through which information can be collected very easily. Professional as well as personal data can be collected by creating a Google Form and even a quiz can be created and evaluated. A spreadsheet can be created automatically of the collected data and automatically saved in Google Drive. Google also validates the Responses automatically in form of charts which can be copied and pasted wherever required. Many inbuilt themes are available and forms can be customized very easily. Many Add-ons are also available to increase the efficiency of forms. Multiple-choice questions, checkboxes, short answer questions, long answered questions, etc can be created. The form allows us to collect different kinds of uploads including files of jpg, doc, pdf, and even audiovisual files.

Google Classroom : The 'Google Classroom' is a Content Management System, it is a user-friendly tool to facilitate the teaching and learning process in an organized and systematic way, that too paperless. Through it, a teacher can make an announcement to the students, supply the learning material to the students, and can virtually perform all other classroom activities with ease. It helps to organize all the learning material systematically, as everything of GC is automatically saved in Google drive. It helps to encourage the discussion between the students and their respective teachers/instructors. Teachers, like on any other LMS system, may work on GC wherever & whenever, rather in a more convenient manner. It is course management software that is free of cost, easy to use, and an organized way of sharing information resources.

Google Blogger : Google Blogger is a blog-publishing service that allows multi-user blogs with time-stamped entries. It is a free but simplest blogging platform launched in 1999 by Pyra Labs, which was later acquired by Google in 2003. It is a hosted blog platform so no hosting website is required and a person having a Google account can create a blog after following simple guidelines. No technical knowledge or coding experience is required to create a blog using blogger.com as it is quite intuitive in design and setup. It is a very secure and reliable site as it is backed by Google. It is free, anyone with a Gmail account can create a blog using subdomain via blogspot.com, provision of the customized domain is also available on meager payment. It is a very simple and user-friendly platform, no codding and technical knowledge is required to make a blog on blogger. All the features of the plugin are free and included inside itself only. Several templates are available, layout, background are customizable. There is no limit to creating number of blogs with one Gmail and there is no limit on the number of visitors. One can monetize the blog by integrating it with Google AdSense. Blog analytics is also integrated within the Blog settings to assess the blog's traffic and see the content getting the most visits.

Google Site : Google Site is a free service provided by Google since 2008 to create a Website. It gives a very simple and user-friendly option to create and customize the website. The support of google makes it more powerful in this genre. There is no space problem on the google site. The Google Drive cloud space is available for your website whereas others sometimes after creating a website asking for money. The website under google site is available in the search engine of Google.

YouTube : YouTube is a video sharing applications provided by Google. It is a more powerful platform and most acceptable due to the user-friendly platform and is now to be used to showcase creativity and entertainment. YouTube works with a mission 'to give everyone a voice and show them the world'. YouTube is taking care of not only the emotional aspects of one's life but also privacy and freedom. The person may express himself without any fear or any apprehension. Whereas, they may explore their creativity and present it to the world with ease.

Google Meet : Google launched Google Meet in March 2017 for Real-Time meetings and Video Conferencing. It is the replacement of two Google apps Google Hangouts and Google

Chat. One main feature of Google meet is its integration with Google Calendar and Google Contact, which enables one-click meeting calls. Google Meet helps easy video conferencing where participants can share their screen, make presentations and videos, and even record the meetings.

G-Suite for Education : "G Suite" is a "suite of cloud computing, productivity and collaboration tools, software and products". G Suite for Education is used by over 120 million students and educators around the world. It is a product which is first launched on August 28, 2006, by Google as "Google Apps for Your Domain". On October 10, 2006, Google announced an edition for schools, then known as Google Apps for Education as "new ways that educational institutions can use Google technologies to power communication, collaboration and search for their campus communities". "Google Apps for Your Domain" means educational institutions can find a domain for their institution (for example gcg42.ac.in or rmlnlu.ac.in), get professional emails accounts for all their stakeholders & create the website of their institution with Google. According to Google, the G Suite for Education is developed to "Empower learning while getting more time back to focus on your students with flexible, secure, and easy-to-use tools that are free and built for education". It comes with unlimited cloud storage, additional administrative tools, and advanced settings, and 24/7 phone and support from Google Inc. In a way the whole institution comes under one umbrella: uniform email addresses, the administrator has full control to access activities done by the respective email holder and is completely ad-free (G-Suite users do not see advertisements while using the services).

OTHER GOOGLE APPS

Google Calendar : Google launched Google Calendar as a time-management and scheduling calendar service in 2009. It helps users to create and edit events, even setting up reminders and adding location is also possible through this service.

Google Current : Google Current is a service provided by Google with G-Suite. It is a digital bulletin board, which can be used for communication with employees working at the same organization. People can chat, share files, and generally, it is used to stay connected.

Google Drawings : Google Drawing is the drawing tool provided by Google, which can be accessed through the Gmail account. It can be used to create charts, layout diagrams, create flow charts. Like other Google apps, it can be accessed online anywhere and on any device.

Google Duo : Google Duo is a Video Calling app developed by Google. It's free, simple, and works on all devices be it a smartphone or a PC. One can make one to one call or a group call up to 32 participants. One can chat, do a video call or voice call using Google Duo.

Google Jambora : Google launched Jamboard on 25 October 2016 as an interactive whiteboard via Google Cloud. It has a 55" 4K touchscreen display, which can be used to boost students' and teacher's collaboration and engagement. It can also be used for online meetings

Google Keep : Google launched Google Keep on March 20, 2013. It is a note-taking service provided through Google cloud and can be used on any of the devices. It has several tools for taking notes, including text, lists, images, and audio. It can transcript voice recording, it can enable creation, sharing, and collaboration with other people on notes and lists.

Google Earth : Google Earth is a free computer program from Google, which renders a 3D representation of Earth through high-resolution graphics and satellite images. It is the world's most detailed globe.

Google Input Tools : Google Input tool is a free tool, which enables to type in the 90+ language. It additionally memorizes the corrections and helps to create a customized dictionary. It can be used both offline and online.

Google Maps : Google Maps is a real-time navigation tool, which was launched by Google in February 2005. One gets satellite imagery, aerial photography, detailed street maps along with actual traffic conditions. It provides alternate routes, reaching time while traveling by foot, car, bicycle, air, and public conveyance.

Google News : Google launched Google News in 2002 as a personalized news aggregator service or we can say web news service. It provides comprehensive, up-to-date news coverage of the world happenings.

Google Podcasts : Google Podcast Service is a very simple and free podcasting service launched by Google on June 18, 2018, for Android devices. One can listen to the podcasts of the world.

Translate : Google Translate is a free multilingual neural machine translation service, which was launched in 2006 by Google. It instantly translates words, phrases, and web pages between English and over 109 other languages. In one go, it translates 3900 characters only. The beauty of this product is, it also provides the pronunciation, dictionary, and listening to translation.

Vault : Google Vault is the information governance and eDiscovery tool, which is a part of G Suite, allowing customers to retain, hold, search, and export their data. Vault can be used to data in Gmail messages, Drive files, Google Chat messages, Google Meet recordings, and associated chat, Q&A, and polls logs, Google Groups messages, Google Voice messages, and Classic Hangouts messages.

CONCLUSION

Since its inception, Google just has one mission, making our lives easy, and it is successful in it. There are many more applications and extensions provided by Google, but we have listed only those which can be useful for educationists. Almost every application of Google is simple, free to use, and can be used on several devices. There is just a need to use these applications in a smart way.

REFERENCES

My Apps Georgia Southern University Learning Center (2020). What are Google Apps? https://sites.google.com/a/georgiasouthern.edu/google-apps-fac-staff/getting-started/why-google

https://blog.hubspot.com/marketing/google-docs-tips

https://www.brightcarbon.com/blog/google-slides-ulimate-guide/

2

G-Suite for Education

A Lifeline for Educational Institutions

"G Suite" (G-Suite, 2020) is a "suite of cloud computing, productivity and collaboration tools, software and products". G-Suite for Education is used by over 120 million students and educators around the world. It is a product that is first launched on August 28, 2006, by Google as "Google Apps for Your Domain" (Ktoridou et al., 2013). On October 10, 2006, Google announced an edition for schools, then known as Google Apps for Education as "new ways that educational institutions can use Google technologies to power communication, collaboration and search for their campus communities" (Google, 2006). "Google Apps for Your Domain" means educational institutions can find a domain for their institution (for example 'gcg42.ac.in' or 'rmlnlu.ac.in'), get professional emails accounts for all their stakeholders & create the website of their institution with Google. It comes with unlimited cloud storage, additional administrative tools, and advanced settings, and 24/7 phone and support for Google Inc. In a way the whole institution comes under one umbrella: uniform email addresses, the administrator has full control to access activities done by the respective email holder and is completely ad-free (G-Suite users do not see advertisements while using the services).

According to Google, G-Suite for Education is developed to "Empower learning while getting more time back to focus on your students with flexible, secure, and easy-to-use tools that are free and built for education". Educational institutions can transform their total working by incorporating G-Suite for Education in their routine functioning. It comes free of cost for eligible educational institutions. Each G-Suite for Education account provides 10,000 user accounts (Marie, 2020). By using G-Suite for Education teachers and students of an educational institution can work on their own or collaboratively, at any time, anywhere, and through any device, be a laptop, personal computer, or a smartphone.

G-Suite comprises almost all the applications provided by Google. Apps like Gmail, Meet, Calendar, and Currents can be used for communication while Drive for unlimited cloud storage. Apps like Docs, Sheets, Slides, Keep, Forms, and Sites can add-on to the productivity and collaboration among the stakeholders of the institution. Additional apps like Vault and Jamboard are also available for G-Suite account holders. Security of Institutions' data is the added flavor as all the information is saved on Google's data centers. The beauty of Google apps in nothing is to be saved on the desktop or other devices; everything is saved instantly. Furthermore, G-Suite administrators can fine-tune security and privacy settings.

ADVANTAGE OF USING G-SUITE FOR EDUCATION

Free of Cost : G-Suite for Business and G-Suite for Enterprise are paid versions of G Suite, but G-Suite for Education is free of Cost for educational institutions.

Advertisement Free : No advertisements pop up while using the application of Google for G-Suite for Education account holders.

Domain Name : Since every individual of the institute has a common domain name it is very easy to connect via email, chat, and video conference.

Unlimited Storage Space : If an institution has more than 5 users G-Suite for Education enables unlimited space (is shared by Gmail, Google Photos, and Drive) for storage of data on the cloud.

Collaborative work : G-Suite for education helps in enhancement of collaborative work. Teachers and students can work together for anywhere and anytime using Google Docs, sheet, and slide in real-time; Team can be created for teams and projects or different courses, classes, and subject areas and data can be saved in Team Drive.

Google Calendar : Use of Google calendar can help to manage all the tasks of an institution, it can help to create build to-do lists, create task reminders, and schedule meetings;

Centralized Control : The administrator has the power to control users, he can add users, control their activities, and manage all the devices. The administrator can generate audit reports.

Data Security : The administrator can configure security and settings; it helps to keep all the data safe; Google saves all the data on Google Data Centers to keep the user data safe.

Support : The G-Suite of Education account holders are provided 24X7 supports by Google by phone emails & chat.

Smart Search : The G-Suite of Education allows smart search across G-Suite with Cloud Search.

eDiscovery : The G-Suite of Education enables eDiscovery which allows to retain, search, and export the data of emails, chats, and files.

Google Vault : Google Vault comes as a free application with G-Suite of Education and it helps to retain track of the data of the institution on Google Drive, Gmail, Team, group chat, and Google Meet.

SERVICES WITH G-SUITE FOR EDUCATION

The Core Services which come along the G-Suite of

Education are Classroom, Sheets, Slides, Docs, Calendars, Forms, Sites, Drive, Mail, Groups, Jamboard, Currents, Vault, Meet, and Drawings.

The Additional Services which come along the G-Suite of Education are YouTube, Blogger, Earth.

Many Third-party applications go very well with G-Suite for Education which can be installed using G-Suite Marketplace. These applications enhance the usability of Google's basic services. Some of them are SketchUp for Schools, Form Limiter, Autocrat, Pear Deck, Nearpod, Kami - PDF and Document Annotation, Timify.me, Flubaroo, Doctopus, Form Mule - Email Merge Utility, PowerSchool Learning, Classroom Manager, Copy Down, CoRubrics, Auto-LaTeX Equations, GradeBook, ASSISTments App, Classroom Attendance Tracker, Scratch Blocks, Classroom Share, Automagical Forms, Vocabulary.com, TeX equation editor, Problem-Attic Import, Magic Rainbow Classcraft, Edulastic, Quiz Banker from New Visions for Public Schools, Timer + Proctor, Snip, Template Tab by Alice Keeler, Fishbole Video, Magic Digital Badges, Common Core State, Merge Google Documents, Spreadsheets, Formative, Plagium, Multiple Images, YouTube to Google Slides, CLASS-MON, BadgeU, ImExClass, OKIOCAM for Google Forms, Essay Metrics, etc.

ADVANTAGE OF G-SUITE OF EDUCATION OVER BASIC GOOGLE APPS

S. No	*Particulars*	*Normal Google*	*G-Suite for Education*
1.	Advertisement	The popping of the advertisements are there	Advertisement Free
2.	Institution-wide email (Common domain)	Not Possible	Possible
3.	Storage	15 GB	Unlimited storage

4.	Google Classroom	No Administrator Control	Full control of Administrator. Google Classroom can be created for all the classes by the administrator only and teachers and students can be added to the individual classrooms.
		No Google Meet link	Google Meet Link in the Classroom itself.
		No Guardian Feature	Guardians are linked to their students and can receive email summaries.
		Plagiarism Check Feature not available	Plagiarism Check Feature available
		Marks feature is there for creating Grade Card	Grades feature is there for creating Grade Card (some extra features are added over Marks).
5.	Google Meet	100 participants can be added in one Meeting	250 participants can be added in one Meeting.
		Live streaming is not possible	Live streaming is not possible up to 100,000 viewers.
		Recording of Meeting is not possible	Recording of Meeting is possible
6.	Migrating on-premise data to G-Suite for Education cloud.	Not Possible	Possible
7.	Shared calendars	Not Possible	Possible
8.	Team Drive	Not Possible	Possible
9.	Google Vault	Not integrated	Integrated
10.	eDiscovery	Not integrated	Integrated
11.	Currents	Not integrated	Integrated
12.	Admin Console	No	Yes to control the activities of all the account holders.

13.	Security	No	Powerful backup and cybersecurity functionality is possible.
14.	Google's support	Yes	More Powerful Support.

ELIGIBILITY FOR G-SUITE FOR EDUCATION ACCOUNT

Google offers G-Suite for Education for free to all educational institutions (School, College, University) globally who qualify to certain criteria. These Criteria are :

- The educational institution should have verified not-for-profit status.
- It should be government-recognized, should be accredited with some government agency, and should be delivered nationally or internationally-approved courses at primary, secondary, or higher education.
- If Homeschools (where children don't go to school whereas they are taught by their parents or private tutors) they must be verified by a state homeschool organization.

But the institutions which get academic or operational funding from national or local government, such as military academies and public libraries or even nonprofit organizations, are not given access to the free G-Suite for Education Account (Google, 2020).

STEPS TO APPLY GSUITE EDUCATION ACCOUNT

1. Go to G-Suite for Education signup area : *https://gsuite.google.com/signup/edu/welcomeandclick 'Next'*

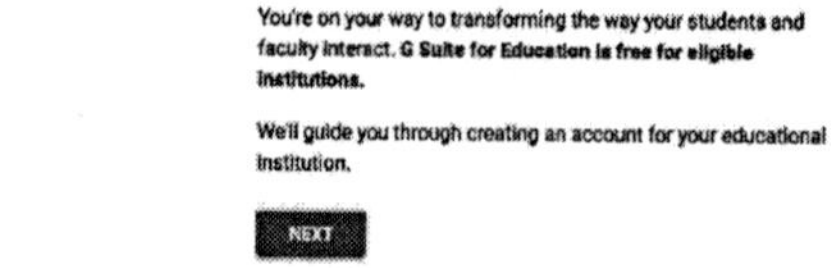

https://usefyi.com/g-suite-for-education/

2. You will be asked to give details of your institution, now fill the name of the Institution and type of the Institution and click 'Next'.

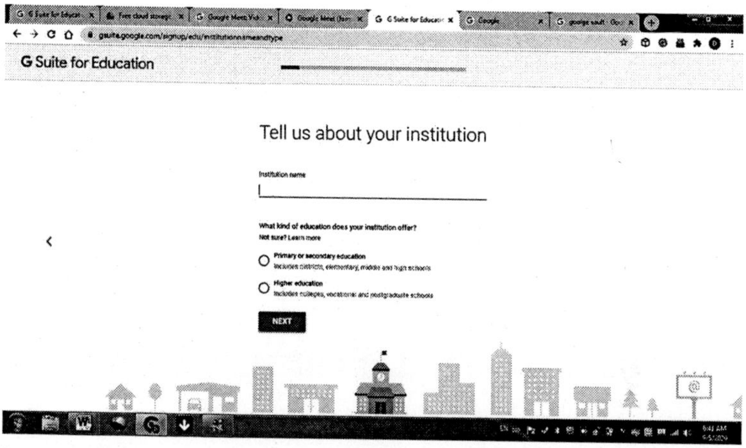

3. In the third step, you will be asked about the website URL of your institution and also the size of your institution. Give the website address of the Institution and details about the number of Students and click 'Next'.

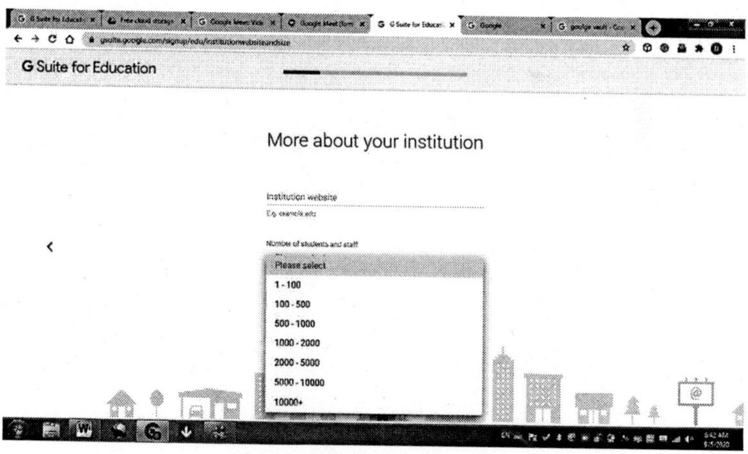

4. In the next step give the location and phone number of your Institution and click 'Next'.

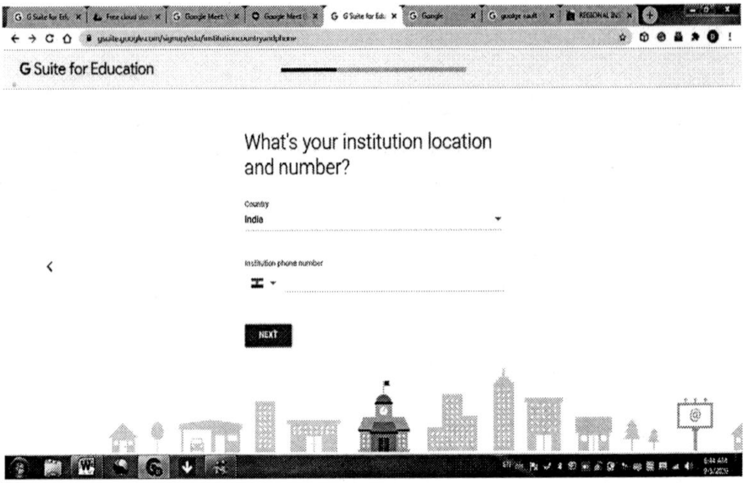

5. In the next step give address details of the institution, click 'Next'.

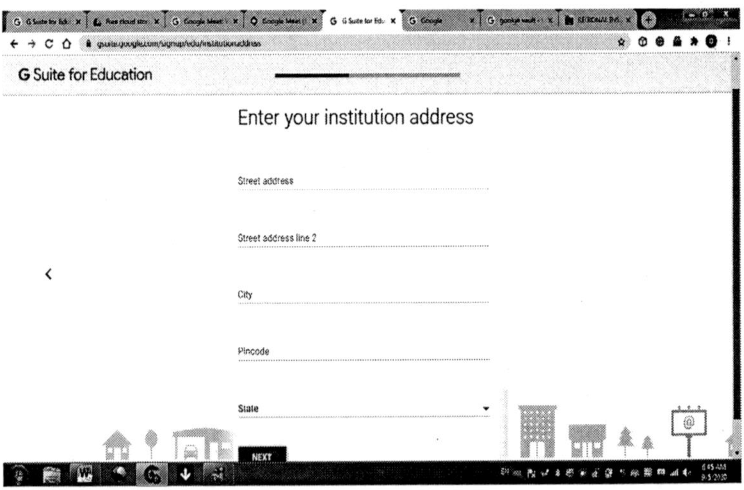

6. In the sixth step give the contact information (First Name, Last Name, and current email address preferably of the Admin) and click 'Next'.

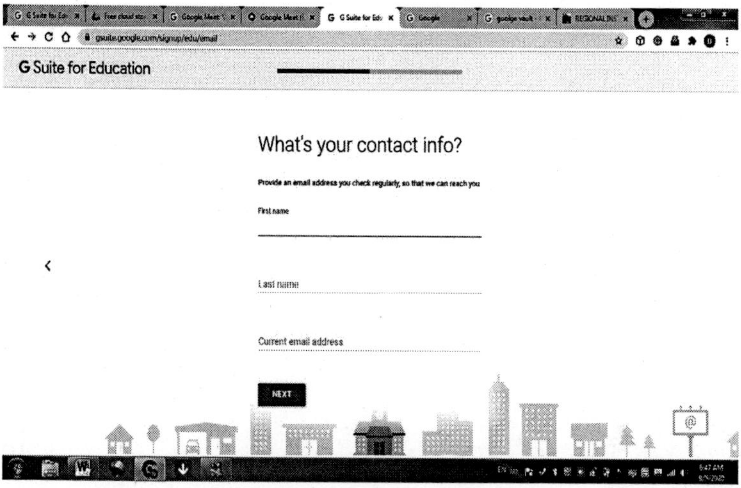

7. Now you are required to give Institution's domain name (desired one), click 'Next'.

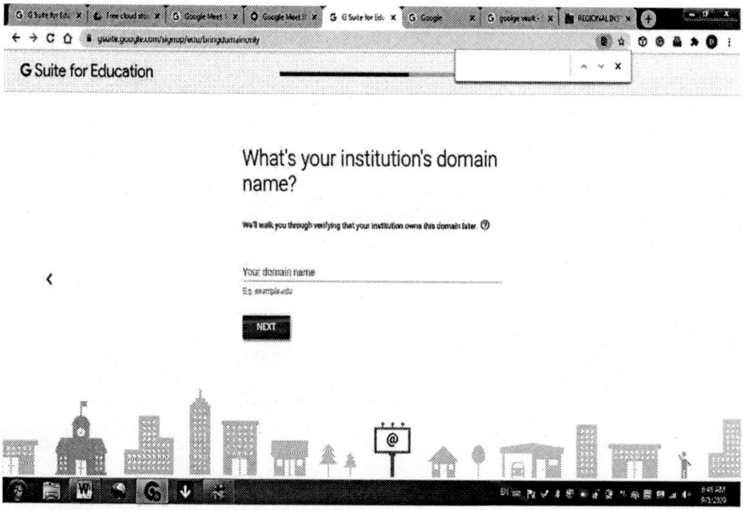

8. It will confirm the domain name in the next step, click 'Next'.

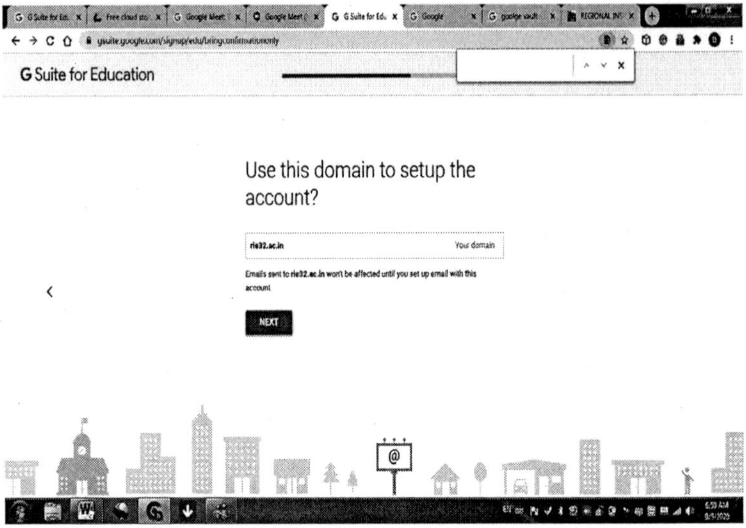

9. In the 9th step, it will ask for signing details: username and password you want to use, click 'Next'.

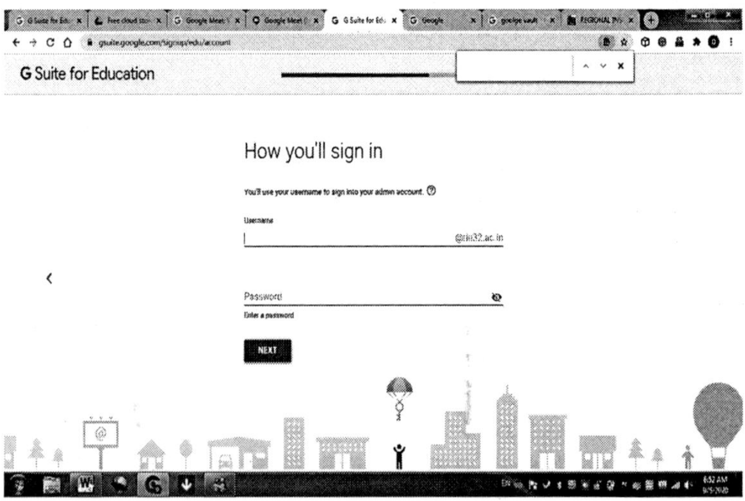

10. You can skip the next step, click 'No Thanks'

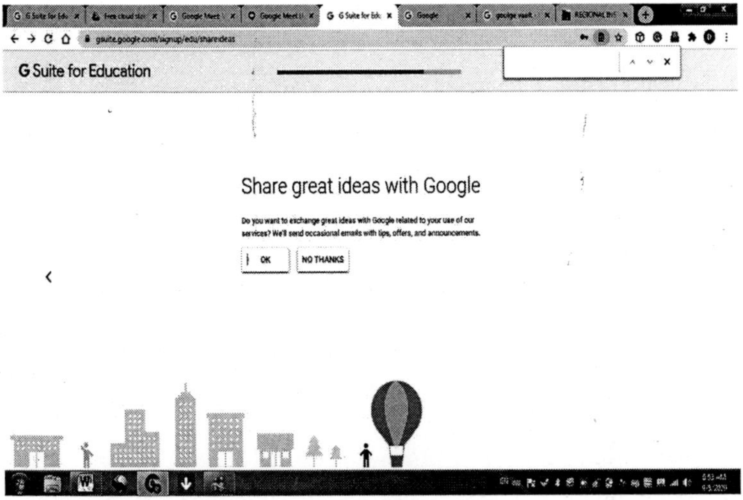

11. In the next step, it will ask for consent (terms and conditions). Click on Agree and continue.

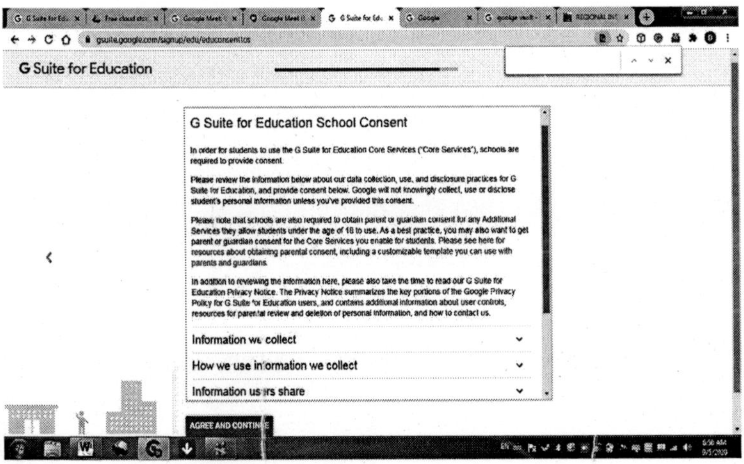

12. In the last step, "Review the G-Suite for Education and G-Suite for Nonprofits Agreement terms and click **Agree and create account**" click on the 'I'm not robot captcha'.

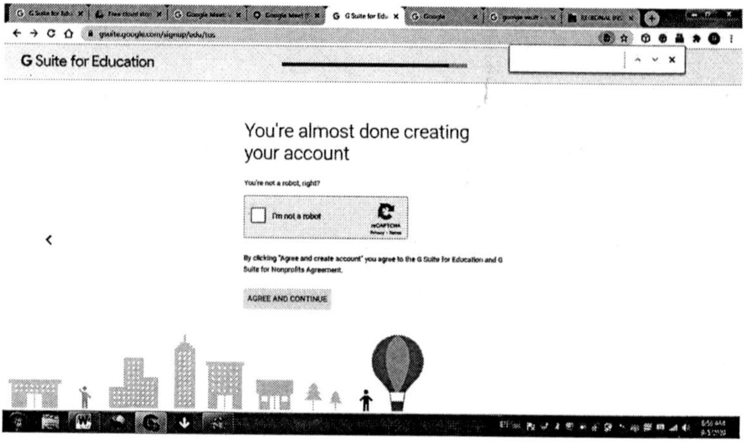

Trail period for G-Suite for Education of 14 days will be started.

ACTIVATING THE ADMIN ACCOUNT

1. The first Step is to enter the setup.

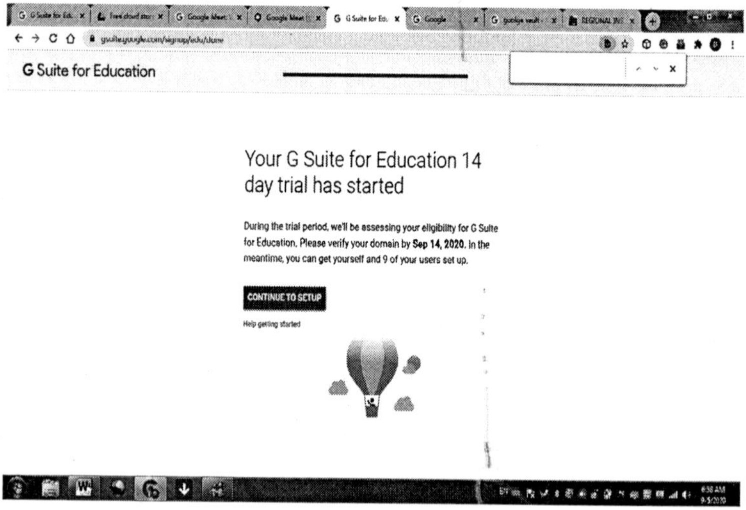

2. The second step is to activate the G-Suite for Education Account.

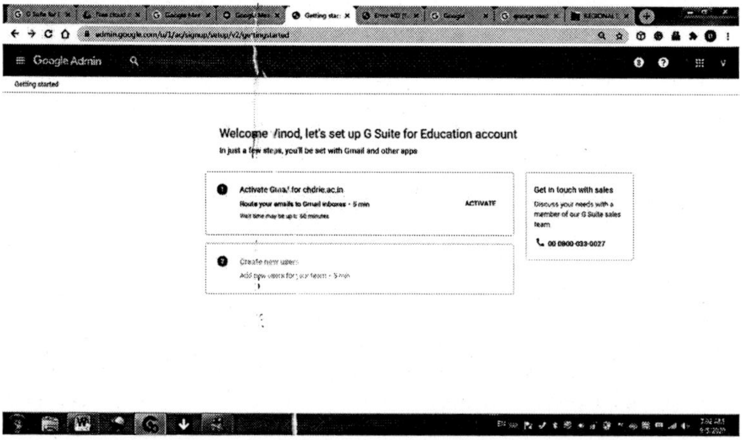

3. In the third step, it will ask for Domain settings, click on continue.

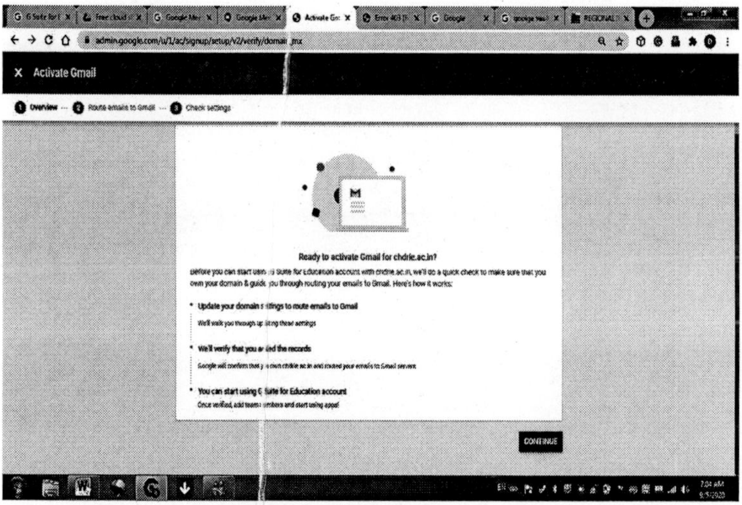

4. To activate Gmail, follow the instructions to update your domain email settings, which are called MX records, click on Activate Gmail.

Let's route your emails to Gmail

To activate Gmail, follow the instructions to update your domain email settings, which are called MX records.

MX records are like a post office for your email. When someone sends you an email, your MX records know how to deliver it to your Gmail inbox. **Learn more**

1. Go to your domain host's website in a new tab

If you're not sure who your domain host is, you can look up your domain host. **Learn more**

2. Sign in to your domain host

Sign in using your domain host's username and password. If you forgot your password, contact their support.

3. Go to your MX records

If you can't find **instructions for your domain host**, use these general steps.

Note: If people already have email with your domain (such as *user@yourdomain.com*), create their user accounts in the Google Admin console *before* you set up your MX records. That way, they'll continue to receive email.

a. In a second browser window or tab, sign in to your domain host account. **Help me find my host.**
b. Go to the section where you can update your domain's MX records. It might be called something like **DNS Management**, **Mail Settings**, or **Advanced Settings**.
c. Select the option to add a new record.

4. Add MX records for Gmail

a. From the **Type** drop-down list, select **MX**.
b. In the **Name/Host/Alias** field, enter @ or leave it blank.
c. In the **Server/Mail Server/Value/Answer/Destination** field, enter **ASPMX.L.GOOGLE.COM.**.
d. In the **Priority** field, enter 1.
e. In the **Time to Live (TTL)** field, enter 3600 or leave the default value.
f. Click **Save**.
g. Follow these same steps to add the MX records shown in this table. Start from the top of the table and enter as many as you have room for.

MX SERVER ADDRESS	PRIORITY
ALT1.ASPMX.L.GOOGLE.COM.	5
ALT2.ASPMX.L.GOOGLE.COM.	5
ALT3.ASPMX.L.GOOGLE.COM.	10
ALT4.ASPMX.L.GOOGLE.COM.	10

Note: Each address is for a Google mail server. We provide several servers in case one becomes unavailable. Some hosts also require a trailing period at the end of the server name.

5. Get your verification code

qmmvxb2gy4vcw3sv54rlhnhocrrertdhtsn76nqskiq54lsz3ypa.mx-verification.google.com. COPY

6. Add MX verification record

Add another MX record just like you did above. Only this time:

- In the **Server/Mail Server/Value/Answer/Destination** field, paste the **MX verification record** (ends in mx-verification.google.com) you copied above.
- In the **Priority** field, enter 15.

Tip: If there isn't room for another MX record, remove the last MX record you added above (the last one in the table). Then add this MX verification record.

BACK ACTIVATE GMAIL

It takes about 2 weeks to process an application. Google will verify your domain before they review your application. This verification process ensures that no one else is using this domain for Google services without your permission or sending an email that appears to come from your institution. You need to submit the following information to completely activate a G-Suite for the Education Account:

- Access to the website of the institution.
- Proof of accreditation and educational status.
- Proof of nonprofit status.
- Proof stating nonprofit status.
- Name of the Admin name, contact email (not related to G-Suite account), and title, role, or affiliation with the educational institution.

After the verification process, you will receive an email of approval. Now through the admin console users can be added and an email can be created for every user with the domain of the institution. You can do other settings like set up apps, and access advanced features, such as mail migration.

G-SUITE ADMIN CONSOLE

Admin Console is the heart of the G-Suite of Education. The person who has access to Google Admin Console, the Administrator can manage all the G-Suite services of the institution. Admin Console makes setup and management of G-Suite for Education fast and easy. Administrators can "Manage user permissions", can be given access to all or specific apps, and can add users or delete users, manage individual permissions, and remove user access. Administrators can fine-tune security and enable privacy settings.

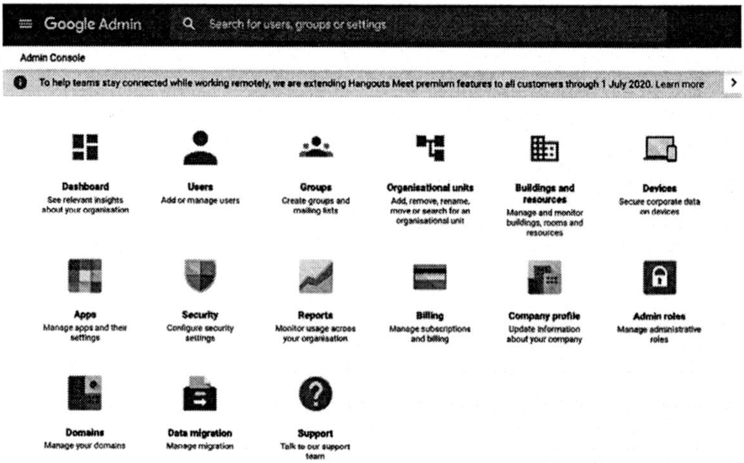

G-SUITE ADMIN CONSOLE

Core Services of Admin Console of G-Suite for Education (Anacleto, 2020)

S. No	*Feature*	*What you can do with it*
1.	Dashboard	The dashboard of the Admin console is the place where the administrator can view insights (detailed metrics on the Institution's G-Suite usage), notifications, and recommendations about the institution.
2.	Users	This control helps to manage users of the institution. The administrator can control 'Account & contact information' and 'Associated Google+ profile' of all the users. Administrators can enable G-Suite and services to an individual user. The administrator can add or remove users, put users in organizational units, or groups and assign admin roles to users who can help to manage the G-Suite services. The administrator can also see the last login and email usage of a particular user.

3.	Groups	Google Groups can be created by the administrator for the team working on a project or an event or various departments. By creating groups, the member can send a single email which will be received by everyone in the group. An online discussion forum can be created in which group members can discuss anything. This is another way to enhance collaboration in the institution.
4.	Organizational units	Administrators can create Organizational units to apply settings or policies to a specific set of users. By default, all users of G-Suite for Education of an Institution are placed in the top-level (parent) organizational unit. Various departmental units can be created in an institution; work-profile-wise units can be created; units of students, teachers, and administrative staff can be created to provide each group access to different sets of G-Suite services. This is an important service as it will help to give access to information and tools to various organizational units. For example, students' units will not be allowed to create a Classroom; in the same way, some apps may be restricted to a specific unit.
5.	Buildings and Resources	Through the Buildings and Resources features in the Admin Console, the administrator can manage and monitor the buildings, rooms, and resources of the institution. The administrator can add the details of the building of the institution, address and location of the building, details of various floors, rooms, and various campuses. Details of various resources and equipment of the institution have to be also added to this section. This will help the users to know about information like the where auditorium of the institution is located and what all facility it has, or where the canteen or washrooms are located, where is the library located and where are various laboratories of the institution and what equipment and facilities are available there.

6.	Devices	Through this control of the Admin console, the administrator can add and manage all the devices through the G-Suite Education accountholder login to the account. Whenever an accountholder login to the G-Suite account through any browser the device is automatically registered to the admin console. Now admin can see which device is used, what are the operating system and other signing details also. This management can help the administrator to get information about every login and he can use this data to make policy regarding the management of various devices in their institution. He has the power of even restricting any device to log-in.
7.	Apps	Through this service, the Administrator can manage settings for all the apps and services of the G-Suite of Education account of the Institution. Administrators can control domain-owned apps like Gmail and Google Calendar as well as the third-party apps; the administrator can decide which apps can access sensitive G-Suite data. The administrator can either restrict access to most G-Suite services or leave them unrestricted/ Trust specific apps so they can access restricted G-Suite services/ or Trust all domain-owned apps. Administrators can decide which third-party apps can be downloaded by the users, the administrator can also give limited access to certain apps or even block some apps.
8.	Security	Through this service, the administrator can manage all the security features for the G-Suite account of the Institution. Administrators can do the basic settings, password monitoring, API reference, Set up single sign-on (SSO), Advanced settings. In the G-Suite for Education, an extra layer of security to the data can be enabled for the users by asking them to authenticate with a verification code as well as their password.
9.	Reports	In this section, the administrator can track the

	usage of all the G-Suite services and apps available in the Institution Account. Administrators can monitor every user's activity, status, storage statistics, and also security. This section is organized by Highlights, Security, Apps Usage Activity, Account Activity, and Audits. This section helps to generate audit reports to see how the users manage and use G-Suite services.
10. Billing	This section informs about the account subscriptions. Since G-Suite for Education is free, this section is less of use. But if the Institution wishes to upgrade to the paid plans of G-Suite they can see the upgrade plans available to them in this section. Administrators can add payment methods, print the invoices, and even cancel the subscription.
11. Company Profile	The administrator can customize the details of the Institution (name, native language & time zone) and can set G-Suite communication preferences (specify the email on which email Google should send alert). The administrator can review all the information related to the Institution G-Suite of education account and can accept compliance agreements (GDPR, HIPAA). The administrator can upload the logo of the institution, details about the Institution, and provide the URL of the institution.
12. Admin roles	This section allows the administrator to assign administrative roles to other users of the Institution. The administrator can promote an existing user to the level of a Super Administrator, which will allow him to perform all tasks on the Google Admin Console. The administrator can also assign a custom role to a user which will enable him to do the task assigned to him. Administrators can also choose pre-built admin roles like Groups Admin or User Management to make the management of G-Suite account.

13.	Domains	Through this control, the administrator can add and remove the domains which are linked to the institution's G-Suite account. The domain can be added as a domain alias or a secondary domain.
14.	Data migration	Through this feature of the G-Suite, a user can import data from his previous emails to his G-Suite account from previous emails. Contact, Calendar, and emails can be imported using this service. To migrate, information like migration source, connection protocol, and the credentials of the account user is required.
15.	Support	The G-Suite administrator has to sign in as an admin to get online, phone, and case support for specific help topics. Help is provided by the Google team to solve the issues about the use of Google apps. Institutions can also request for the addition of any missing feature at the Feature Idea in Google Cloud Connect. This support is provided 24X7 to G-Suite of Education account users.

CONCLUSION

G-Suite for Education is a free service to eligible educational which is entirely online and can be accessed anywhere and anytime (24/7) with Internet connectivity. It is a very authoritative service by Google that integrates almost all tools of Google with full administrative control. This service provides tremendous benefits, in the realms of the educational environment. It is a very smart way of collaborating, communicating, storing, and accessing data. It is a great opportunity for teachers and students to work collaboratively using interactive and easy-to-manage tools of Google. This will ultimately help improve the entire teaching and learning process. The availability of Institution-wide email to every staff member can lead to ease in communication, it makes the contact information look much more professional than general addresses. In a way by subscribing to the G-Suite for Education, an Institution can have a secured email setup that is completely ad-free and has access to unlimited storage space.

REFERENCES

Anacleto, S. (2020). *Managing the G Suite Admin Console | DragApp.com.* https://www.dragapp.com/blog/g-suite-admin-console/

Google. (2006). *Google Announces Education News at Educause – News announcements – News from Google – Google.* http://googlepress.blogspot.com/2006/10/google-announces-education-news-at_10.html

G-Suite. (2020). Google Workspace. In *Wikipedia.* https://en.wikipedia.org/w/index.php?title=Google_Workspace&oldid=995489981

Ktoridou, D., Eteokleous, N., & Dionysiou, I. (2013). Google's Applications for Undergraduate University Courses: Tools for Sharing, Communication, and Collaboration. In *Handbook of Research on Didactic Strategies and Technologies for Education: Incorporating Advancements* (pp. 632–645). IGI Global.

Marie, P. (2020). *Everything You Need To Know About G Suite for Education.* https://usefyi.com/g-suite-for-education/

3

Google Meet

Tool for Educators and Students

The real-time audio call to real-time video call is the revolution in the transformation of telecommunication technology. The end-user is always mesmerized to experience a video call rather than an audio call to their known and loving ones. The technology works where you do not have hope to connect and interact in tough times like the COVID-19 pandemic. The pandemic has disturbed routine job skills and life to interaction, communication, and dissemination of verbal communications. Education is one of them which is one of the most affected domains where education from playgroup to higher studies are seriously been taken up as a challenge to engage infants and students in their studies and research. The online teaching-learning is the answer to the problems created during the pandemic in imparting education throughout the world. The technology here stands firmly in assisting the students and teachers in their teaching-learning. Video conferencing tools is one of the technologies to be adopted and delivered.

The efforts were started right from the 1870s through audio wires and in 1927 a video phone to create a history in sending images and video call (Wolfe, 2019). The present era is fully dominated by the communication technologies in imparting participation right from business to social to personal to education. The various video conferencing platforms emerged in the last two decades to serve the expectations of the consumers. Skype, Zoom, WebEx, Gotowebinar, Whatsapp, MS-Team, and Google Meet, etc. are some of the video conferencing application players who changed the entire set of communication during the pandemic period in 2020.

WHY VIDEO CONFERENCING/MEETING

The video conferencing/meetings are responsive to time-saving, space-saving, and manpower saving. The programmes may be organized for a large number of participants irrespective of geographical and time constrain. The sharing of the screen, use of a whiteboard, and sharing of presentations and other media files empower online teaching and learning. It not only saves time but also resources. Flexibility is the key to the success of the use of video conferencing/meeting applications.

BACKGROUND

The year 1927 was the revolution where two-way audio and one-way video communication was made in New York by Bell Labs. The continuous development was made by various engineers and companies in bringing audio/video-enabled communication devices. In this line, Cornell University was the first to introduce 'CU-SeeMe' first-ever video conferencing application in 1992. Skype launched video calls for 25 persons as a free version in 2003 which service was hugely used by the executive and personnel of various companies for their day-to-day updates. They are :

1. Free: Jio Meet, GoBrunch (G2, 2020)
2. Hybrid (Free & Paid): Google Meet, MS-Teams, Zoom, GoToMeeting, Cisco Webex, Google Hangouts, Skype etc.

3. Open Source (Miller, 2020): Jitsi, Mconf, Jami, ezTalks Cloud Meeting

GOOGLE MEET

Google meet is one of the most reliable and secure video meeting applications. It is free and as well as enterprise version is available to everyone who has an e-mail account with google i.e. Gmail account. The video meeting may be joined or hosted on Brower or Windows, android, and iOS version Google Meet application. These may be downloaded from Google Play Store or Apple Play Store. The Google Meet was started for the Google Hangouts application which initially allowed for instant chatting and then extended for video calling and communication purposes. The Meet was launched by Google in March 2017 which was capable to host a meeting for 30 participants only (*Google Meet - Wikipedia*, 2020). It was extended now up to 100 users for the free version and educational institutions, it is 250 users.

FEATURES

Low-light mode

Google Meet has recently added a new feature to work on low lighting conditions. The AI of the application auto-adjusts the sorrounding lights for better video quality. But it is available for the mobile version only.

Tiled layout for larger calls

Google has enhanced the 'Tiled Layout' feature. In a larger audience, 16 participants along with the shared presentation may be seen on a single screen. It gives you new attraction among the Meet users.

Noise cancellation

Noise cancellation is one of the best features in video meet applications available with Google Meet. It makes the call and meets distraction-free from some noises of background like vehicle noise or horn noise etc. Google is offering this feature to its G-Suite and Education versions.

High-quality video content with audio

Through this feature, high-quality audio/video content may be shared by sharing the Chrome Browser tab. This facility is available only with a Chrome browser.

End-to-End Encryption

Security and privacy are one of the aspects of online audio and video call or meeting. Every user is very attentive towards privacy and Google meet gives end to end encryption of each message and call. The security of google is one of the best features which makes google meet the best in video call class applications.

Anti-hijacking

Online data sharing is vulnerable to many risks also. Data protection and data privacy are one of the challenges in an online meeting environment. The Meet provides counter abuse measure technology which protect data and also from any kind of hijacking. It gives two step verification to avoid any kind of misuse of the system. Google Meet follow international set of data protection policy to ensure safe and secure use of online video meeting facility.

Collaborative

Google meet is collaborative with Microsoft outlook calendar and google calendar to schedule meetings and send alert messages to participants automatically. It also gives space to google drive up to 15GB for free users and unlimited to enterprise users and 100GB to workplace licenses.

GOOGLE MEET LICENSES

Google meet is available in three versions or licenses-

Free

It is known as a personal use license which is free and available for 100 participants. It means that only 100 participants may participate in a meeting but an unlimited meeting may be scheduled. The Gmail account is a prerequisite for any google meet license. The maximum time slot for each meeting is one hour which is maximum for other meeting software like Zoom, WebEx, etc. Live streaming and recording is not available.

Workplace

Google Workspace Essentials license is the paid version. It is used for business purposes. A maximum of 150 participants may join a meeting. A meeting may be continued up to 300 hrs. The recording of the meeting is available whereas live streaming to this edition is not available.

Enterprise

Google Workspace Enterprise is also known as G-Suite for Education edition and workplaces. It allows 250 participants in a meeting and the meeting may be continued up to 300 hours. It also extents live streaming. The meeting may be recorded too.

ADVANTAGE OF GOOGLE MEET

The pandemic has given a chance to apply more online and digital environment in facilitating communication and education over the internet. The video conferencing software companies are updating their meeting software to meet the requisite challenge in the domain. Bas Van Kaam (Kaam, 2020) brought his third comparative chart in reference to the remote video conferencing and online meeting software.

The online meeting software is having more or less the same features, but the pricing model is varying as per user and the purpose for which the meeting software will be used. Google Meet is one of the best for academic purposes in their league. It gives not only to share and record the meetings but also seamless attendance and distribution of assignments functionality gives it an upper hand to their competitors.

Features	Microsoft Teams	Google Hangouts	amazon Chime	webex	zoom	GoToMeeting	slack
Clients / Cloud / Mobile	Web, Windows, Mac, Android, iOS and Linux	Web, Windows, Mac, Android, and iOS	Web, Windows, Mac, Android, and iOS	Web, Windows, Mac, Android, and iOS	Web, Windows, Mac, Android, iOS and Linux	Web, Windows, Mac, Android, and iOS	Web, Windows, Mac, Android, iOS and Linux
Monthly subscription	Yes. Monthly and annually (discount applies)	Yes. Monthly and annually (discount applies)	Yes. Monthly, daily, and pay as you go	Yes. Monthly and annually (discount applies)	Yes. Monthly and annually (discount applies)	Yes. Monthly and annually (discount applies)	Yes. Monthly and annually (discount applies)
Add-ons	Voice calling and audio-conferencing plans, & Bookings (MS application)	No. Features depend on chosen license and plan	Business calling, Voice connector, Dolby Voice Room & Outlook	Call me international	Cloud storage, Video webinars, join by toll free numbers & call me	Join by toll free numbers and call me, Video webinars	Unlimited number of integrations with other third party apps
* Max users in video	4	10	16 desktop, 8 mobile	Not sure. Look here	49	25	15 video call
* Max users in meeting	250. Optional online events up to 10.000 attendees	250	250	1000 for Meetings and 3000 for events	1000	3000	Video calls only (15). Unlimited users in chat
HD video quality	Yes	Yes	Yes	Yes	Yes	Yes	No, through 3rd party only
Raise hand option	No. Coming later in 2020	Yes	No	Yes	Yes	Yes	No, through 3rd party only
Background noise red.	No. Coming later in 2020	Yes. Ambient noise filtering	No. Only through Dolby Voice Room	No. Warnings only	Yes. Auto reduction feature	* No. Through third party apps. Like Krisp for example	No, through 3rd party only
File sharing	Yes. 365 suite	Yes. Gsuite	Yes. Own solution	Yes. Own solution	Yes. Own solution	Yes. Plugins plus own solution	Yes. Plugins plus own solution
Recording optional	Yes	Yes	Yes	Yes	Yes	Yes	No, through 3rd party only
* Cloud storage	Yes. 25 TB per Team plus 10 GB per license	Unlimited. Or 1 TB per user with less than 5 users	No	10 GB of Cloud storage	1GB of MP4 or M4A Cloud recording	Unlimited Cloud recording storage	1 TB per team member
Whiteboard function	Yes	Yes	Yes	Yes	Yes	Yes	No, through 3rd party only
Free version	Yes, and a free trial as well	Yes, and a free trial as well	Yes. Free trial available	Yes, and a free trial as well	Yes. No free trial	No. Free trial available	Yes, and a free trial as well
^ Price range user/month	€ 4.20 - € 34.40	€ 5.00 - € 23.00	€ 3 per day - € 15 monthly	€ 12.85 - € 25.65	€ 13.99 - € 18.99	€ 10.75 – contact sales	€ 10.75 – contact sales
REST API available	Yes	Yes	Yes	Yes	Yes	Yes	Yes
Support options	24/7 support, phone and web. FastTrack deployment support	24/7 support, phone, web, and e-mail	24/7 support, web	24/7 support, web	24/7 support, phone, web, and chat	24/7 support, phone and web, live and on-demand training	24/7 priority support (web) with four-hour first response time

* Based on license type. Combination of voice, chat, and video. * Max number of users that can be seen by everyone at the same time. Based on most expensive license.
* Krisp is a 3rd party background noise reduction tool, works with all solutions out there, on Windows and Mac. ^ Pricing can vary per reseller / partner. Teams is part of Office 365 license.

Thursday, April 9, 2020 - Twitter @HusvanKasm

Google Meet is using their multi-purpose software like Google Calendar, Google Drive, YouTube, Google Classroom, etc. which have integrated each other and gives seamless and powerful video conferencing environment. It gives every freedom to share, retrieve, and impart education without any extra financial Burdon.

GOOGLE MEET FOR LIBRARIES

The digital environment is empowering libraries and library services at every moment. Libraries are always happy and meaningful while interacting with their users. It doesn't matter either it is online or offline or personal interaction but sharing ideas and knowledge is the key to the success of libraries. During the COVID-19 unavoidable circumstances, the students are not able to visit the library and the library does not have the opportunity to serve them personally. But, the Online medium is the savior in this situation.

Libraries are playing a major role in organizing various information awareness programmes for their users and others too. Video conferencing meeting application software tool is to handle the demand of users. Google meet is helping in organizing Library Orientation and Awareness Programmes/ Training programmes and book exhibitions and book release event. The study materials, contents, notices, circulars, and other information are been distributed and shared in real-time over the google meet by the libraries. The optimum use of Google Meet is empowering libraries and its users almost every day in dissemination, training and knowledge sharing activities.

HOW TO USE GOOGLE MEET

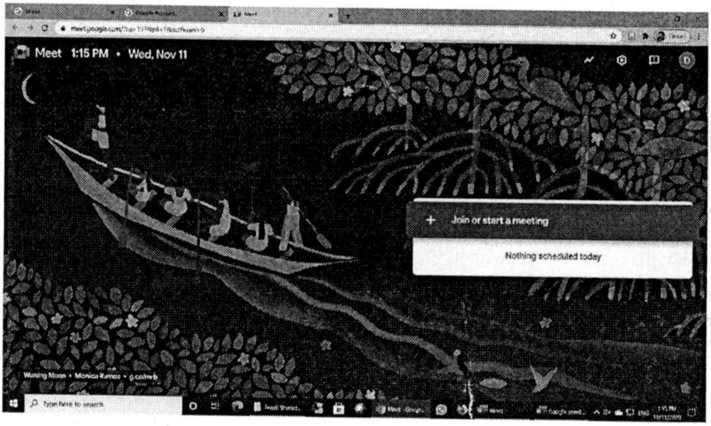

JOIN OR START A MEETING

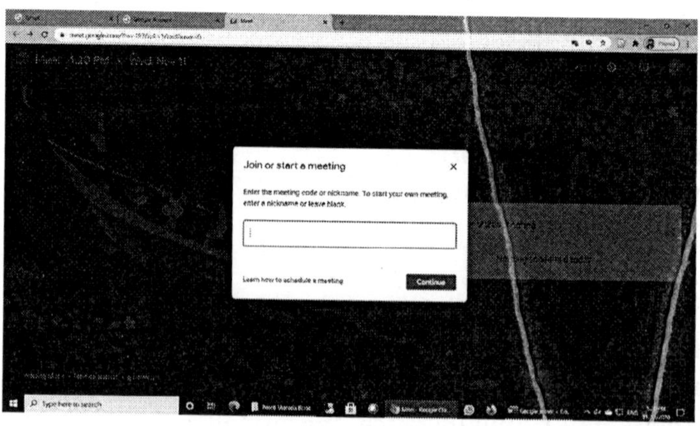

After all basic setting acceptance, the host and participant may join the meeting. The meeting may also be scheduled through Google Calendar or Microsoft Outlook. The link updated to the calendar may be directly used to start or join a meeting who have a Gmail account. But, other than Gmail account users, they will get a meeting code and password through which they may join. The meeting may be joined through the app or on the browser.

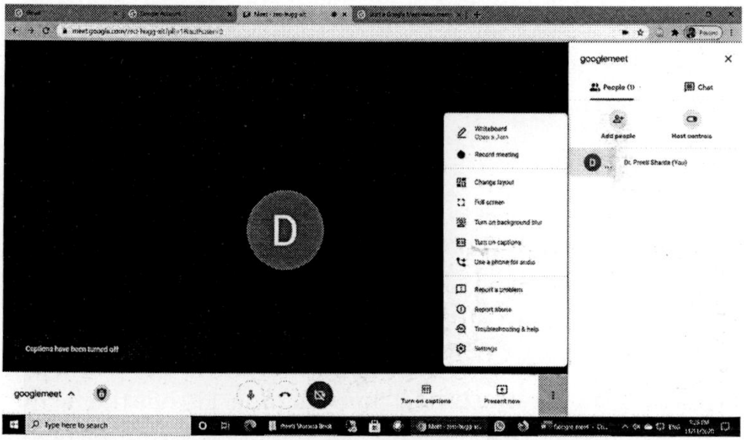

Whiteboard is used to write something on the screen for students and participants. Google meet is using the 'Jamboard' application to facilitate the whiteboard to its users. A touch screen panel is required to use it. It is a wonderful feature which gives the experience of blackboard teaching.

Record Meeting is used to record the meeting for further use. But, caution is that the meeting may be recorded with the permission of all the participants. By default, the meeting is recorded to the host's google drive account.

Change Layout gives four options for a better screen look. They are auto, tiled, spotlight, and sidebar. Auto is the default view of the screen, tile is used to bring all the participants on the screen but only 16 participants may be seen on the screen at one instance, the spotlight is used for the presented view of a full view of the presenter whereas sidebar is used to accommodate participants along with host/ presenter view.

Turn on background blur option is used to make the background blur for a better presentation where you are in a place which is not good for the video meeting.

Turn on captions (CC) is used to share views on the screen instantly during the meeting.

Live Streaming in google meet is not available but it can be done by using some open broadcaster software (OBS). The host must have a channel on his YouTube account. The OBS has to be linked with google meet screen and YouTube Chanel.

PRESENT NOW

Your entire screen : It is used to share the entire computer/laptop/mobile screen to show to the participants. It is very useful to switch one content to another. It reflects all the content which a screen has.

A Window : If the presenter is working with many windows at the same time in his machine. He has the facility to choose anyone it from the opened windows to present before the participants.

A Chrome tab is used to represent contents available within the google application family. Host/presenter may show the content of Gmail or google drive through this application instantly.

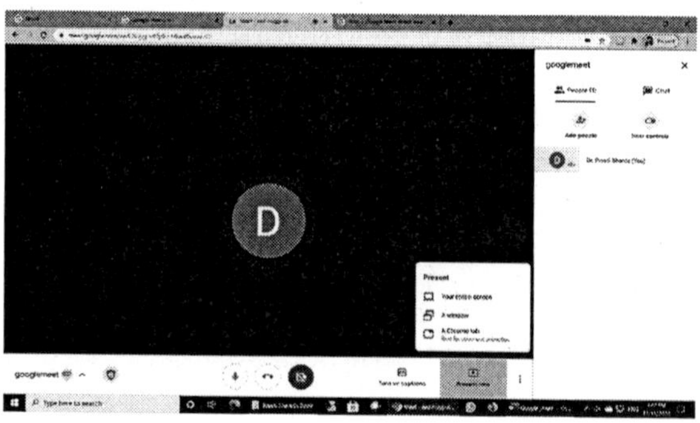

HOST CONTROLS

It is more like to restrict participants to share their screen or mute and unmute to all the participants or specific participant.

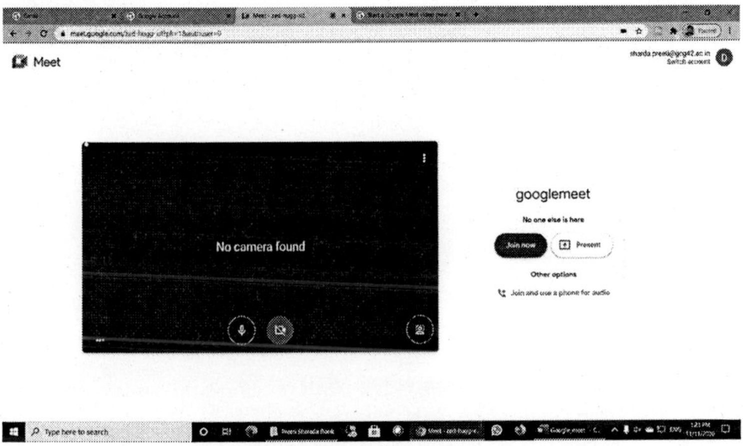

TRACK MEETING QUALITY AND STATISTICS

It is used to control the administrative dashboard of the google meet. The administrator may assign a role to different users in a meeting.

Setting : Is used to set audio and video quality setting during the using of the Google Meet. It may ask using computer auto and camera or any other device which is attached for the purpose in the computing device. By default, it is using the primary source of audio/video.

CONCLUSION

The technology-driven society is always looking for opportunities to use and impart information communication technology in their success. Education is one of the stockholders which requires much attention and use of ICT in imparting research and education. Like other technologies, the video conferencing of video meeting software technology is going to be very instrumental in conducting real-time class teaching, online training programmes, and workshops to reach to the un-reach. Google meet is one of the best video meeting or conferencing software which may be used for the teaching and learning process. The integrated software and seamless functionality and user-friendly features are making it the most popular among every age group. The Google Meet application software is going to be very helpful in imparting education from primary to higher education.

REFERENCES

G2. (2020). *Best Free Web and Video Conferencing Software in 2020*. G2. https://www.g2.com/categories/video-conferencing/free

Google Meet – Wikipedia. (2020). https://en.wikipedia.org/wiki/Google_Meet

Kaam, B. van. (2020). *The ultimate remote video conferencing and online meeting software cheat sheet 3.0*. https://www.basvankaam.com/2020/04/03/the-ultimate-remote-video-conferencing-and-online-meeting-software-cheat-sheet-3-0/

Miller, S. R. (2020). *The Best 8 Free and Open Source Web Conferencing Software Solutions*. https://www.goodfirms.co/blog/best-free-open-source-web-conferencing-software-solutions

Wolfe, E. (2019). *The 150 Year History of Video Conferencing: 1870 – 2020 [Timeline]*. https://www.lifesize.com/en/video-conferencing-blog/history-of-video-conferencing

4

Google Classroom

for Teaching and Learning

Google Classroom is a free web service developed for educational institutions that aims to simplify creating, distributing, and grading assignments. It is one of the facilities offered by Google like Gmail, Chrome, Drive, etc. Google officially launched Google Classroom on August 2014 for Google's G-Suite for Education program. Google developed the Google Classroom under the motto "to help teachers create and collect assignments" and was based on the principle "educational tools should be simple and easy to use". In 2017, Google opened the Classroom for all personal Google users. However, it gained popularity in August 2018 when it made major changes in the classwork section. It is regularly updated. Several developments like improvement of grading system, organizing the material by 'Topic', dragging and dropping of topic & improved assignment grading, etc have made Google Classroom a real hit. Today over 100,000,000 Teachers use Google Classroom Worldwide to send out assignments and communicate with students.

It is Learning Management Software. It is a technology in the classroom designed to provide a single dashboard to unify instructors' use of other Google apps. It helps create a virtual classroom space. It is basically designed to ease teaching-learning process and make it more systematic. Google Classroom is designed to help teachers to devote more time to teaching rather than involving in other activities such as make material accessible to students and at the same way, students should spend more time learning rather than collecting material from teachers (Shaharanee et al., 2016). The primary purpose of Google Classroom is to streamline the process of sharing files between teachers and students. It is a platform to share preparatory content, surveys, and worksheets with the students and also provide a place for class discussion. Google Classroom brings large number of students together into one virtual classroom to ensure that all are receiving the same links and material. It focuses on three key areas: pose questions, make announcements, and set assignments. It is course management software, which is free of cost, easy to use, and an organized way of sharing the information resources.

Google Classroom is available as Desktop Version as well as Mobile App for both IOS and Android devices and can be downloaded from the app store.

ADVANTAGES OF USING GOOGLE CLASSROOM (Iftakhar, 2016)

- Creating a Google Classroom is very easy. Anyone with a Gmail can just log in and create the classroom.
- Managing Google Classroom is also very easy. Teachers and students do not require any formal training to work on it.
- It is a mode of online education available 24/7. Time constraints in the classroom is no longer a problem.
- It bridges the geographical gaps and can be accessed by everyone from any part of the world having access to the Internet.
- It is free and secure. Since provided by Google it is very much secured. While downloading the app Google

never asks to share any of the resources. It contains no ads and Google never uses teachers' content or student data for advertising purposes.

- One of the biggest advantages of the Google Classroom is the folder 'Classroom' created in Google Drive of the user be it is the teacher or the student and every activity of the Classroom is being saved in this folder. So none requires extra space in any devices. Secondly, since the data is saved in Google Drive it can be accessed from any device or any place.
- Google Classroom saves time of teachers and students. It helps to avoid repetitive jobs. The material of one class can be used in future classes. Everything is virtual so time wasted in printing or delivery is saved.
- It is a kind of digital organizer, which organizes every activity of the classroom that too digitally.
- The beauty of the Classroom is it makes everything paperless so it is Eco-friendly also. From creating the content by teachers, creating assignments, conducting an examination, and giving the mark sheet, everything is paperless (Roche, 2017).
- The complete setup of Google Classroom is very Flexible. Teachers have full control over the classroom. They can add students, easily delete and recreate classes and students only get what they need.
- Google Classroom is designed so beautifully that integration with Google's popular tools (doc, slide, sheet, form, drive) can be easily done.
- Google Classroom is developed to encourage the 'Flipped Classroom' scenario. Teachers send the students material in the format of text, ppt, video, and suggested readings. Students see the material and complete the assignments (Subandi et al., 2018). Teachers and students meet each other through the virtual forums created to discuss the topics.

- Google Classroom enables real-time feedback and grading. Teachers can return the assignment, tests, and quiz to the students virtually along with the comments and marks. The students can also interact with their peers and teachers in the Stream.
- Google Classroom enables ease in giving material (Texts, videos of the classes, link to other material from the Internet, and other instructional media) to the students. Teachers can also arrange the material topic wise, which they can use for future classes also.
- Google Classroom makes it simple for the students to take notes in Google Docs or Keep them for future use in Google Classroom. The real advantage of Google Classroom is that it allows all of these material to be gathered in one place, so everything is easy for students and teachers to find. At the same time, it can be accessed from any device at home, at school, or in the library.
- Google Classroom enables to conduct virtual discussion groups. This format encourages interaction and collaboration.

MAIN TABS OF GOOGLE CLASSROOM

Main tabs of Google Classroom are Settings, Stream, Classwork, People, and Marks

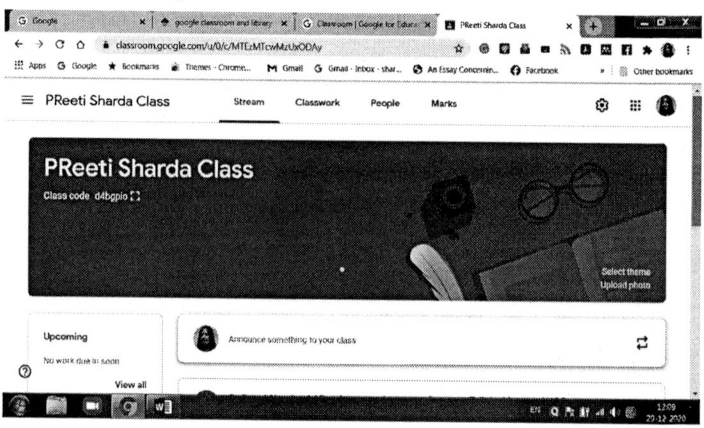

- The setting is for
  - Adding Class details: Name, Section, Room, Subject.
  - View, share, modify, and disable the class code.
  - Deciding about student's privileges in Stream whether to enable or disable students commenting.
  - Adjust how classwork appears on the stream, it may appear with all the attachments and details or as a condensed notification; or a teacher can hide classwork notifications on the stream altogether.
  - Choose whether deleted items to appear for other teachers or not.
  - Deciding about Marking Calculations and Marking Categories: A teacher can control the grading system for the classroom from this part of the settings. Turning to grade off completely is also possible and a teacher can get the grades automatically calculated by using total points available or by weighting grades by category. A teacher can also design various grades matrix within the settings.
- People is an open list of teacher and students' profile information. It is basically to manage co-teachers and students. It can be used:
  - To view the strength of the classroom or to add and remove co-teacher or student.
  - Co-teachers can be added by sending the invite from the People tab through email. There are two ways to add students to class one is by sending an invite and the other is giving the Class code, a student has to join a classroom by entering the class code.
  - Co-workers or teachers added to the class can do everything that the owner of the class does but he

or she cannot delete the class.

- The Stream is the Conversational hub of the Google classroom. It is like a chatbox. It can be used for:
  - Making Announcements for upcoming events
  - Facilitating Interaction between students and teachers
  - Adding Material from Google Drive and device
  - Providing Links or YouTube Video
  - Creating a Virtual Forum enabling discussion between peers
  - Announcements of assignments created on the Classwork tab
  - It also highlights the upcoming event or assignment.
- Classwork provides Teachers with a definitive space to post assignments. A teacher can send the classwork to all the students of a class, a selective student in a class, or all the students of all the classes owned by the teacher. It can also be used for:
  - Arranging topic-wise material of the class
  - Create an assignment, to be submitted through google doc slide or sheet
  - Posing a question to the students
  - Creating a quiz using Google Form and attaching it in classwork
  - Sending material to the students
  - A teacher can also reuse the classwork post from this tab
  - Once the student submits the assignment, the teacher can check it and return the students.
  - A teacher can also see in the tab that to how many students the assignment was assigned and how

many students have returned it.

- Grades feature of Google Classroom is called Marks, it is to give feedback and grades to the assignments of the students. It is for:
  - Creating the grade card of the students
  - To keep an eye on the students who have not completed an assignment.
  - Weigh all the assignments and show the students an average based on the weightings.

ROLE OF TEACHERS AND STUDENTS IN GOOGLE CLASSROOM

Google Classroom is meant for teachers and students. Teachers perform some of the processes and the students can do the rest. If we sum-up

- Teachers can :
  - Create and manage classes
  - Control and Manage classroom members
  - Create content
  - Share resources
  - Give assignments
  - Interact with Class
  - Give real-time feedback and grades
- Students can :
  - Track classwork and materials
  - Share resources
  - interact in the class
  - Submit assignments
  - Get feedback and grades.

STEPS TO WORK WITH GOOGLE CLASSROOM

1. Login : Google Classroom is available free for anyone who uses a Gmail account. It can be accessed by any web browser (classroom.google.com), one has to login with a Gmail account. From here, follow the steps for creating the classroom. It will ask you to continue and accept terms and conditions.

2. Creating a Classroom : Once the teacher enters the Goggle classroom, he can either join a class or create a new class. Teachers can add various classes and sections as needed. They have some freedom when it comes to basic classroom design, such as class themes. After the class is set up, then it is time to sign the users up. A teacher can add co-teachers or students through email invite or class code. At this point, the Google Classroom is ready for use.

3. Settings : Once the class is created and students are added, a teacher may decide to adjust the class settings to control what students can do and how grading works.

4. Create Classwork : Now the teacher can Add material, create a topic, Create a grading system, and create assignments.

5. Assign Classwork : Once the assignment is created, a teacher should make an announcement in Stream, a notification is automatically sent to the students about it.

6. Completion of Classwork : Students need to complete their assignment on time and return it to the classroom

7. Grade assignments : Once the classwork is received back a teacher should check, give marks and feedback, and return to students.

EDIT, DELETE, OR ARCHIVE A GOOGLE CLASSROOM

There are provisions in Google Classroom to Copy, Edit, Archive or permanently delete the class. A Teacher can edit the classroom setting at any point in time; he can make a duplicate class if he needs to use the same material in the other class. He can achieve the class at End of Quarter/Semester/Year. Archiving preserves materials, discussions, and posts, but restricts new interaction in the class. The teacher and the users can view an archived class; however, no one can edit or add anything to the class until the teacher restores it. A teacher can permanently delete the class if it is not needed anymore, however, all files are still available in Google Drive to view and edit.

GOOGLE CLASSROOM AND LIBRARIES

Google classroom can reflect and focuses on visual approaches. It conveniently enables the sharing of material. It facilitates content creation and ultimately leads to the development of critical thinking of the students, which is the ultimate aim of today's' education system. Google Classroom provides librarians with a definitive space to deliver reading material, post assignments, organize Quiz (Survey) and take feedback from its users (Izenstark & Leahy, 2015). Libraries can organize virtual library tours, orientation programmes, Course-based, subject-specific tutorials, which are developed and delivered in partnership with academic staff. Libraries can supply Instructional materials such as YouTube videos, website links, PDFs, and items from Google Drive accounts. They can conduct surveys by devising quizzes to gauge and test knowledge. They can also launch the discussion forums and chat to stimulate debate and discussion, leading towards book talks, launching of new services, or deciding about new acquisitions and subscriptions for the library. Google Classroom can also help in uploading and working collaboratively on papers, reports, documents to encourage analytic thinking, developing guides to resources, producing online tutorials, for example evaluating resources, getting the best from the internet, and avoiding plagiarism. Libraries are a natural home for Information Literacy. Planned sessions through Google Classroom can reduce the burden on the library professionals. This extension of Google is relatively simple. Google Classroom can streamline the delivery of materials with students in one-time and multi-meeting classes. Ultimately, it will change the stereotype perception towards the library, help to promote the librarian's visibility on the campus and facilitate a good relationship between librarians and faculty members of the institution.

REFERENCES

Iftakhar, S. (2016). Google Classroom: What works and how? *Journal of Education and Social Sciences*, *3*, 12–18.

Izenstark, A., & Leahy, K. L. (2015). Google classroom for librarians: Features and opportunities. *Library Hi Tech News*.

Roche, C. (2017). *Taking information literacy lessons into Google Classroom | Heart of the School*. https://heartoftheschool.edublogs.org/2017/01/30/taking-information-literacy-lessons-into-google-classroom/

Shaharanee, I. N. M., Jamil, J. M., & Rodzi, S. S. M. (2016). Google classroom as a tool for active learning. *AIP Conference Proceedings*, *1761*(1), 020069. https://doi.org/10.1063/1.4960909

Subandi, S., Choirudin, C., Mahmudi, M., Nizaruddin, N., & Hermanita, H. (2018). Building interactive communication with Google classroom. *International Journal of Engineering & Technology*, *7*(2.13), 460–463.

5

Google Chrome

More than a Web Browser

Google Chrome is a free cross-platform web browser and was launched by Google in 2008. It is the most used web browser today and has a 68% worldwide browser market share (StatCounter, 2020). All Google services work better with Google Chrome. It is more than just a web browser. It manages its system resources differently than other browsers. According to Google, it never developed Chrome to replace the available Web browsers like Microsoft's Internet Explorer and Firefox, rather it developed Chrome in order "to advance the usefulness of the Internet by including features that would work better with newer Web-based technologies, such as the company's Google Apps (e.g., Calendar, Word Processor, Spreadsheet), that operate within a browser" (Hosch, 2020). Essentially it is an operating system that functions in the cloud. It helps in synchronization of all the Google services and Google accounts. It enables tabbed browsing, and helps in automatic translation and spell check of web pages. Chrome is configured in such a way that its updates are downloaded automatically. Chrome is a very fast and reliable browser that has numerous built-in and add-on benefits.

To make maximum use of Google Chrome sign in with your Gmail account. It will help the user to save and sync bookmarks, history, passwords, and other settings to his Google Account. Even if he uses another device to use chrome he will get similar settings. Slight changes in Google Chrome can make it more usable and user friendly.

FEATURES OF CHROME

Incognito Mode : This is a private browsing option provided by Chrome to increase the privacy of the user. A user wants to browse in an isolated sandbox web session. He needs to Ctrl+Shift+N (Windows, Linux) or Shift+N (macOS X). In this way, a user can browse privately other people who use his device won't see his activity. In a way, he will get temporary control over his browsing history and session identity, because when he will close the browser, his logins and browsing history, Cookies and site data, and Information entered in various forms will be deleted. However, downloads and bookmarks will be saved, and his activity might be visible to the websites he visited, his employer, or school if he is logged in Chrome with his official email and his internet service provider. He can exist mode by the 'Exist Incognito' button in the right-hand side corner of the menu bar of Chrome.

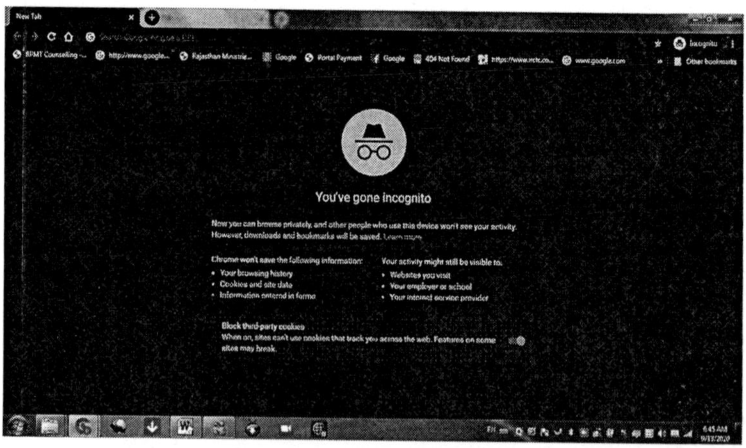

Incognito Mode in Chrome

Omnibox : Google Chrome also features an integrated address bar/search bar, called the Omnibox. The address bar of Google Chrome is more of a search box; it is an Omnibox that enables searching more effectively and efficiently. It does everything, be it doing a quick calculation or finding meaning. Some of the searching tips:

To search within a website : type the name of the website from which you need information and press the Tab key. The address will change into a search box for the particular website. Now you can type your keyword, you will be getting your desired search results.

Smart Lookups : Chrome helps you to look for or define the meaning or originating of a particular word from the page you are reading. Just select the word or phrase for which you want the information and drag it to the address bar and click enter. A new page will be opened and you will find the desired information. You can do it by selecting the word and then right-click and then search in Google.

Use chrome as Timer : Type Timer and a time in the Omnibox (timer 10 minutes) a timer window will be opened

Getting whether of a Location : Type Weather and ZIP code or name of the city, chrome will show you the time of the city.

To translate a word or a phrase : Type Translate followed by the word or phrase and then the desired language in which you want to translate, you will get the desired translation.

To get directions : If you desire to get a map of direction from one place to another then type map and location 1 to location 2 (Map Chandigarh Lucknow), you will get the desired direction.

To do mathematical Calculation : Type directly the equation in the address bar and to get the desired calculation done

Data Conversions : If you desire to Change a currency on it or whether from Celsius to Fahrenheit then write change followed by value units to be changed (change 30 degrees

Celsius to Fahrenheit) you will get the desired values. For Area, Data transfer, Digital storage values, Energy, Frequency, Fuel, Economy, Length, Mass, Plane, angle, Pressure, Speed, Volume, etc. you can use 'Unit Converter'. Type Unit converter in the address bar and now you put the values to be converted and chose the unit of the conversion from the drop-down menu.

Get Definition : to get the definition of any word writes define in the address bar followed by the word.

Find My Phone : By writing 'Find My Phone' in the menu bar you can find the present location of your mobile phone, you can ring the phone even it is silent, you can secure the device and erase all the content from the device if you think it is lost.

Tab : In computing, a tab is a second or further page that can be opened on a web browser. In Chrome, a user is allowed to open as many as 100 tabs.

ORGANIZING TABS

Tag Grouping : This feature allows the user to organize tabs, label them, and color code them, he can collapse tab into groups and expand them.

Pin a tab : This feature helps to keep your important tabs on the left and it will also reduce the tab icon size.

Mute a tab : We can mute a tab from the menu to stop the sound from a particular tab.

Some Commands to manage Chrome Tabs:

- Ctrl + T : To open a new tab
- Ctrl + W : to close the current tab
- Ctrl + Shift + T : To open the last tab
- Ctrl + L : To highlight whatever's is there in Omnibox
- Ctrl + Tab : To move towards a tab to the right
- Ctrl + Shift + Tab : To move towards a tab to the left
- Alt+Home : To Open your home page

Menu Bar : Menu Bar is used to do all the settings of Google Chrome. It can be accessed by clicking the "three vertical dots" at the top right of the Chrome browser window. They look like this:

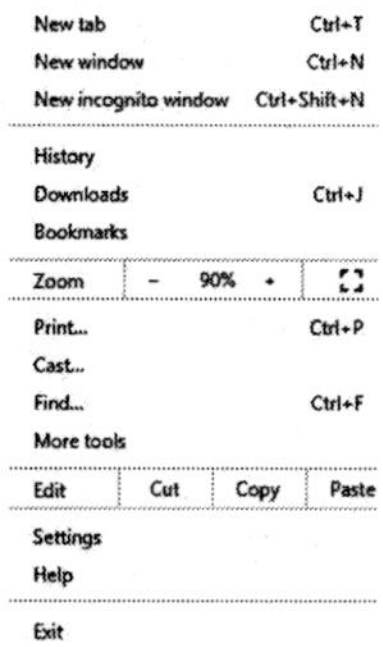

Chrome Menu Screenshot

The menu bar has seven sections:

- First Section is for managing Chrome's tabs and windows (to open New Tab, New Window, and New Incognito Window);
- Second Section has 'History (recently-closed tabs and windows on user's synched devices)', 'Downloads (list of the recent downloads)' and 'Bookmarks';
- The third Section helps to Zoom in and Zoom-out the Chrome Windows
- The fourth Section includes 'Tools', which includes 'Print', 'Cast', 'Find' and 'More tools' (which includes 'save page as', 'create shortcut', 'clear browsing data, 'manage extensions'; and use Chrome's internal 'Task Manager, User can access Chrome's extensive and ever-growing 'Developer Tools' kit.)
- The fifth section is for 'Edit' which includes Cut, Copy, and Paste on the address bar.
- The sixth section is for 'Settings', and 'Help'.
  - Settings includes: 'You and Google' (tells about user account in chrome);

- 'Autofill' (manages Passwords, Payment methods, and phone numbers, email addresses, and shipping addresses);
- 'Safety Check' (Settings regarding safe browsing and update the Chrome);
- 'Privacy and Security' (Through this menu item, a user can clear browsing data: history, cookies, cache, and more; do settings and get information about Cookies and other site data; can see the blocked third-party cookies; do settings about the security of chrome against dangerous sites); and know about the controls of what information sites can use and show (location, camera, pop-ups, and more));
- 'Appearance' (Setting about what will be the theme of chrome, how it will look like; settings about a specific webpage will open when chrome is opened and when New Tab page opened; settings about showing bookmarks bar below the address bar for easy access; setting the font size and user can even customize fonts and page zoom);
- Search engine (Settings about the Search engine used in the address bar and which will be the default search engine and what are other search engines saved in Chrome);
- Default browser (Making the Chrome as the Default Web Browser);
- On startup (User can decide about which page should be opened when Google chrome is opened. Choices are-Open the New Tab page, Continue where you left off or to Open a specific page or set of pages;
- Some advanced settings are also there which include: Languages (default language and allowing

spell check and autocorrect while entering search in Omnibox); Downloads (default setting about location where user has to save downloads, settings can also be done to chrome to ask where to save each file before downloading); Printing (adding printers for cloud print); Accessibility (adding Captions and other accessibility features); System (decision about continuing running background apps when Google Chrome is closed or to use hardware acceleration when available and computer's proxy settings); Reset and clean up (decision about restoring settings to their original defaults and clean up the computer);

- Extensions (this feature is to manage the extensions and apps added to Chrome, user can see the details and even delete the extensions and shortcut of apps);
- About Chrome (This tells about the version of Google Chrome, and from here also user can get help with Chrome or report an issue to Chrome developers);

• The seventh section is to Exit from Menu Bar

Bookmarks : If you want to save some particular site for future reference or you have some favorite site you can click on the start button in the extreme corner of the Omnibox and 'Bookmark the Tab', or click 'ctrl+D'. To retrieve the Bookmarked site to the Settings menu and click Bookmark. You will find all the list of all the bookmarked sites

Chrome Web Store : Chrome Web Store is to add apps, extensions, and browser themes for Google. With these additions, users can do more with Chrome. Users can install free items from here and for the paid apps provision of payment is also made at Chrome Web Store. The Chrome Web Store will always give information about available apps and extensions by the user's browser language and location.

Users can personalize the looks of the Chrome window by changing the themes. Many themes are available in the Chrome Web store of which some are free and some are paid.

Shortcuts of the Google Apps can be added to Chrome for their easy access to Open Chrome. To add a shortcut to any Google app, navigate to the website in the address bar, click on the menu button, click on click 'More tools' and then click on to Create shortcut (enter a name for the shortcut) and click 'Create'. The app will be added to Chrome and can be accessed by clicking on the ⠿ icon in the extreme left corner of the Chrome web page.

Many software can be added as Extensions to Google chrome to increase its usability and functionality; these are the programs that extend the capabilities of the Chrome Browser. Extensions for Google Chrome perform functions such as providing instant access to popular websites, displaying news feeds and linking the browser to reference resources, adding new features to existing web apps, getting relevant links and information on pages, getting timely notifications about certain events. The shortcut of these extensions appears in the address bar of the Chrome browser and also at https://chrome.google.com/webstore/category/extensions. There are about 190000 extensions in the chrome. These extensions are categorized as 'Runs Offline' or 'By Google', 'Free', 'Available for Android, and 'Works with Google Drive'.

Categories of extension in Google chrome: accessibility, blogging, by Google, developer tools, Sports, Fun, News and Weather, Photos, Productivity, Search Tools, Shopping and Social & Communication

To add an extension, open the Chrome Web Store, look for the extension to be added, click on 'Add to Chrome', approve permission, click the 'add extension' option.

A user can install extensions with one click. If an

extension is not required anymore, a user can remove it from the browser. For removing an extension open menu, click "Tools," and then click "Extensions" to open a new browser tab displaying all of the Chrome extensions presently installed. Now click on the "Uninstall" link under the extension which is to be removed. It will open a new window titled "Confirm Uninstallation".

Customize Chrome Browser : Chrome provides a provision of customizing the Chrome Browser, changing the background information, creating shortcut which appears on the main screen and changing color and theme. Icon is located in the extreme right lower corner.

Cast Your Screen : Chrome has an inbuilt feature of casting. Either right-click anywhere in Chrome to prompt a pop-up cast window or in the menu bar choose Cast, Chrome will automatically search for the device for Casting

Google Image (https://images.google.com/) : An extension of Google Images can be added to the Chrome Browser to do image Specific search. The service is provided by Google since 2001 which helps users to search the World Wide Web for image content. A user can find an image on a particular subject or he can do a reverse image search. Google Reverse Image Search allows a user to visually similar images from around the web. If a user wants to publish details of a particular image, he can also search in the Google Image Search.

Google Scholar (https://scholar.google.com/) : A button of Google Scholar can be added to Chrome Browser from Chrome Web Store to do Academic Search. A user can search scholarly material from academic publishers, professional societies, online repositories, universities, and other educational web sites. Users can search for information on all the disciplines which is published in the form of articles, theses, book abstracts, and court opinions. Not only these users can create a profile and they can keep track of citations to their articles. Users can search scholarly articles and they get the option of either get the citation details (in the MLA, APA, Vancouver, Chicago, Harvard format) and see who has referred the particular saved article. Users can create their library by click on save it will be saved in 'My Library', this feature helps users to save their favorite articles, they can organize them topic-wise. The editable citation can be directly exported to a citation manager like BibTeX, EndNote, RefMan, and RefWorks.

Fast Advance Google Search : Many tools are available in Google for searching the web, but sometimes it can be too time-consuming. By enabling 'Fast Advanced Google Search' is a Google Chrome extension users can provide quick access to these advanced tools. After downloading and adding an extension click Alt+G, it will open a pop-up where searching can be done.

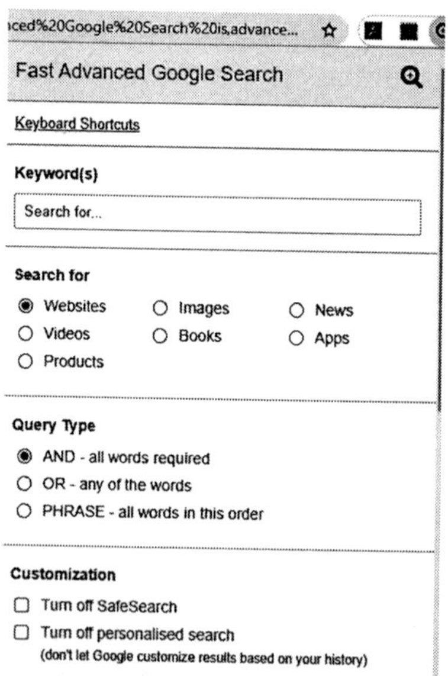

Fast Advance Google Search (Part I)

- **Search For :** Search can be limited to Websites, Images, News, Videos, Books, Products, and Apps.

- **Query Type :** Search can also be limited by Boolean Operator – 'AND' (All words are required in the retrieved document) and 'OR' (Document comprising of any the keyword can be retrieved) and Phrase (All words of the query should be there in the same order) is also possible.
- **Customization :** Customization of search is also possible by turning off Safe Search and turn off personalized search.

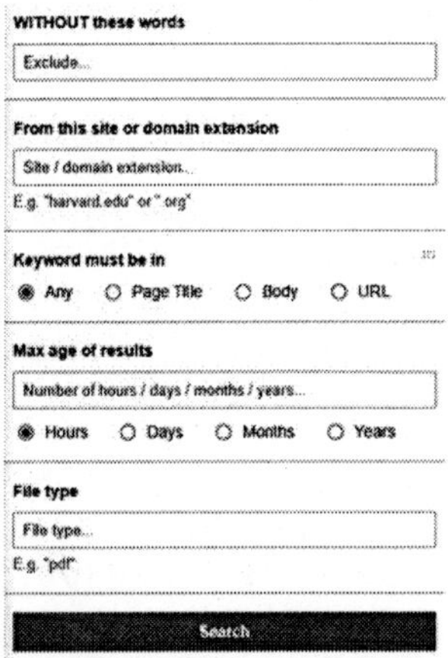

Fast Advance Google Search (Part I)

- **WITHOUT these words :** The user can also exclude some of the words from the search. It serves the purpose of the Boolean operator 'Not'.
- **From this site or Domain extension :** Site-Specific search is also possible; the user can retrieve the document from a particular website or domain extension. Users can also state that the retrieval should be from the specific website only like "pushed.ac.in" or "Edu", etc.
- **The keyword must be in :** Keyword search can also be limited to anywhere from the web or title only or body text only or URL only.
- **Max age of results :** Search can also be limited with the time of the document published on the web. It can be

limited to 'N' Number of Hours or Days or Months or Years.

- **File type :** This setting helps the user to search for a particular type of document, user has to write the extension of the filetype (doc and docx, html and htm, odt, pdf, xls and xlsx, ods, ppt and pptx, .txt.)

CONCLUSION

Google chrome is a free web browser and it enhances the functionality and compatibility of other Google products like Gmail, Google Drive, and Google Calendar. It is very fast and stable and easier to browse. Omnibox, provision of a large number of extensions, bookmarks shortcuts of other Google services has made it the most preferred web browser of Internet users. It is available for all of the major desktop operating systems as well as Android and iOS. Chrome just makes the workflow of many a lot simpler and more accessible. Users who sign in to their Google accounts can sync their tabs, bookmarks, browsing history, and passwords across all of their devices running Chrome. Customization of the appearance of the chrome with favorite themes, font, and colors, add flavors to Chrome. What makes chrome the best web browser is the protection against malware.

REFERENCES

Hosch, W. L. (2020). *Chrome | Description, Features, & Facts | Britannica.* https://www.britannica.com/technology/Chrome

StatCounter. (2020). *Desktop Browser Market Share Worldwide | StatCounter Global Stats.* https://gs.statcounter.com/browser-market-share/desktop/worldwide/#monthly-200901-202005

Chrome Web Store (2020). https://chrome.google.com/webstore

6

Google Office Management

Programmes Tool for Teaching and Learning

Google has many application software but out of all their application tools, are specifically made for Office Management. Google Document (docs), Google Spreadsheets (sheets), and Google Presentations (slides) are the Web-based application to create official documents provided by Google to create, edit, share, and print documents. Many templates are made available. Real-time collaboration is possible using any device. Whatever is done in these documents is automatically saved in Google Drive. Google doc is "an online word processor to create and format text documents"; Google sheets "an online spreadsheet application to create and format spreadsheets and charts"; and Google slide is "an online presentations editor to create visual presentations and shows". Let's discuss the main features of them one by one-

GOOGLE DOCS

Google Docs is an online word processor to create and format documents and work with other people. "It is a cloud-based document solution with real-time collaboration and powerful tools to compose, edit, and share documents". It has ready-made templates for writing Resumes, Letters, Personal, Work, Sales, Legal, Human Resources, Freelance

Management, and Education which can be used while creating a document.

STEPS TO CREATE A NEW GOOGLE DOC

1. Log in to docs.google.com
2. Click on + sign (Blank) alternatively directly open the docs.google.com/create.
3. By default, the document name of the document will be "Untitled document". Click on it and give a name

STEPS TO UPLOAD A DOCUMENT

1. User can upload a document from his computer (format supported are .doc; .docx; .html; .txt; .odt; .rtf).
2. Go to Google Drive, click on new > file upload> go to the location of the file to be uploaded> select the file>open; alternatively, open a new document click on open and browse and upload from the computer.

MENU BAR OF GOOGLE DOC

All the Google office management programmes Google Doc, Google Slides or Google sheet have a traditional menu system with a shortcut toolbar. The menus contain commands grouped by function and the shortcut toolbar below the menu has buttons of commands which are frequently used.

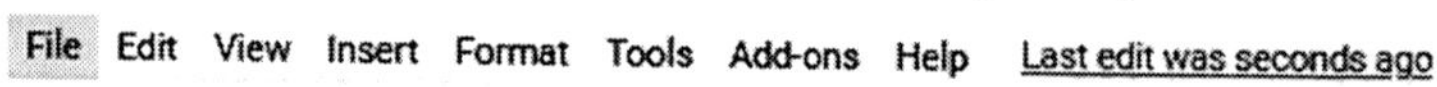

The menu can be minimized also to free up more space to display the document. To hide the menu click on the ^ on the right corner below the share button. This will hide the menu bar, leaving only the shortcut toolbar at the top of the window. To get the menu back click on the same button.

File Menu : The File menu has items that deal with the document as a whole, its sharing, editing, toggling settings.

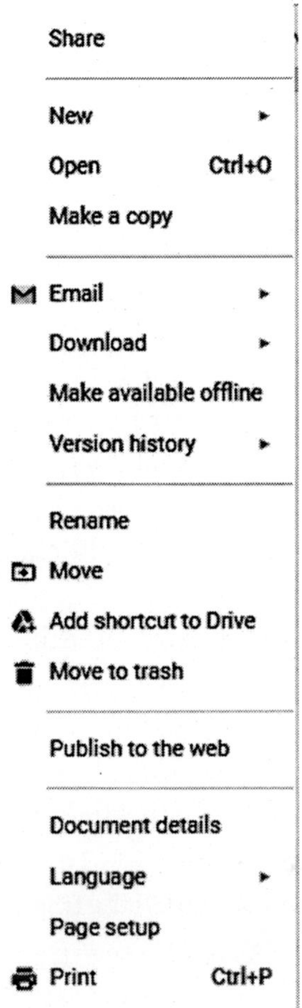

Share : A user can share files with other Gmail holders, can find or download a file

New : He can make a new blank Google Doc

Open : User can open a Google doc or upload a file in doc format for his computer

Make a copy : This launches a dialog that allows a user to make a copy of the existing document by renaming it.

Download as : A user can download the document at his device in one of the following formats:

- Microsoft Word (.docx)
- OpenDocument Format (.odt)
- Rich Text Format (.rtf)
- PDF Document (.pdf)
- Web Page (.html, zipped)
- EPUB Publication (.epub)

Email as an attachment : User can send the document directly as an attachment to the desired recipients

Make available Offline : Document can be accessed offline also if this feature is turned on;

Version history : From here user can see the past iterations of the document (Shortcut to it Ctrl+Shift+Alt+h). User can save the versions as per the change he is making and retrieve as and when required.

Rename : The user can rename the document from here.

Move to : This option allows the user to change the place of the document in Google Drive;

Add shortcut to the drive : this allows to make the shortcut of the document or the device of the user;

Move to trash : This will send the document to the trash. It gives two options: Take out of the trash and go to Docs home.

Publish to the Web : This feature helps to publish a non-editable version which can be viewed via the link or embed the document on the Website.

Document details : This gives the basic information about the document (Location, Owner, Last-Modified and Created on)

Language : The user can choose the language of the document from around 80 languages available.

Page setup : here the size and the orientation of the document can be set.

Print : This is for printing the present document

Edit Menu : Edit Menu has the regular options like 'undo'(ctrl+z); 'redo'(ctrl+y); 'cut'(ctrl+x); 'copy'(ctrl+c); 'paste'(ctrl+v); 'delete'; 'select all'(ctrl+a); 'find and replace' (ctrl+h) and 'paste without formatting'(ctrl+shift+z). Paste without formatting is important to choose to paste anything without keeping the format of the document from where it is copied.

View Menu : View Menu has the option like 'Print layout'; 'Mode'; 'Show ruler'; 'Show Document Outline'; 'Show education toolbar'; 'Show section breaks'; 'Full Screen'. Three modes can be created for a document: Editing for direct editing, suggesting for just suggesting the changes, and for Viewing only.

Insert Menu : An Image, table, drawing, chart, horizontal line, footnote (ctrl+alt+z), special character, equation, headers and footers, page number, break (page break: adding a new page, column break, section break), link(ctrl+k), comment, bookmark and table of content can be inserted in a Google doc. An image can be uploaded from the device or Google Drive and even the web.

Format Menu : Format Menu has options like 'Text', 'Paragraph Styles', 'Align & indents', 'Line spacing', 'columns', 'Bullets& numbering', and 'Borders and Lines'. It also has the option of formatting the 'Headers and Footers', 'page numbers', 'tables', 'and image 'of the documents. The user can clear all the formatting done.

Tools Menu : Through 'Spelling and grammar' spell-check of the document can be done, further 'word count'(ctrl+alt+u) can be used to know the number of pages, words, and characters of the document. Clicking on 'Review suggested edits' (ctrl+alt+o) tells about the suggestion made by other collaborators.

'Compare documents' is provided to the present document with another version of the document from Google drive to track changes and the difference can be attributed to the selected email id.

'Explore' (ctrl +alt+shift+i) brings quick access to the Drive files, web search, images, recommendations, and more. It uses machine learning to try to predict things while creating and composing a document.

Linked objects : This tool is used to "access all linked content (embedded charts, tables, slides, and drawings)" and quickly update them. If the linked object is updated in one document it will be updated in all the documents wherever it is inserted.

Dictionary(ctrl+shift+y) : to look-up words in a dictionary.

Translate Document : this command will create a new document with a translation of your text in the chosen language.

Voice Typing (ctrl+shift+s) : This can be used to dictate text using a microphone and it will be automatically typing in the document.

Script Editor : This tool is for programmers for Script editing.

Preferences : Preferences can be set by using this tool for automatic corrections while typing only. These preferences can be: Automatically capitalize words; Use smart quotes; automatically detect links; automatically detect lists; automatically correct spelling; Suggest action items; Suggest contacts in comments; Show link details. Automatic substitution can also be set.

Accessibility settings : settings can be done regarding turn on the screen reader support to turn on the Braille support (for the third party hardware) or turn on collaboration announcements To know when collaborator enter or exit the document)and to turn on the magnifier support (for third party software).

Add-ons : Many add-ons can be used with Google docs and these add-ons add new functionality and features to Google Docs. By clicking here popup will show the already add-ons and 'Get add-ons', to install form 'G Suite Marketplace'. There are about 100s of add-on which can go with Google doc. A list is provided of some of the best add-ons which can be added:

- **Doc Builder :** Save hours of typing with reusable text snippets;
- **Doc to Form :** It helps to covert a Google doc into Google quiz or Google form;
- **DocSecrets :** This helps to hide certain areas in the document if the document is shared with other collaborators.
- **DocuSigneSignature :** It helps a user to prepare, sign, act on and manage documents;
- **EasyBib Bibliography Creator :** It helps to generate an automatic citation in formats like MLA, APA, Harvard, etc;
- **eNotifications for Docs :** by installing this add-on author gets the email alerts about the changes made in Google doc by the collaborators;
- **Google Docs Offline :** this add on helps to access Google Docs without the Internet;
- **Grammarly :** is the AI-powered writing assistant to suggest the correct grammar and spelling;
- **Lucidchart Diagrams :** it can be used to create flowcharts, diagrams, organizational charts, and more;
- **MathType :** it is an equation editor that helps to type or handwrite mathematical equations in a Google Doc;
- **OrangeSlice–Teacher Rubric :** It helps to generate rubrics for – Grading the students;
- **PlagiarismCheck.org :** It helps to detect similarities;

- **Search & Navigate :** It helps to find and navigate text, headings, bookmarks, images, or tables to any part of the document;
- **Source Documents :** It searches databases of museums, archives, and libraries for images, and embed them in documents;
- **SpeakD :** It is an add-on that gives voice to the written text in the Google Doc.;
- **Translate+ :** This tool helps to translate text into other languages within the document;
- **Writing Habit :** This add-on helps to improve writing skills;
- **Yob – Graph Editor :** It is a powerful graph editor and analysis tool for Google Docs;
- **Help Menu :** This menu helps a user to use the Google Document properly. It gives the option of 'Docs Help'; 'Training'; 'Updates'; 'Send Feedback'; 'Report abuse/ copyright'; 'Private Policy'; 'Terms of Service'; and 'Keyboard Shortcuts'.

On the menubar it is also mentioned when the documents were last edited. This option is very useful to know how long ago the last change was made in the document.

Comments History Button : This tells about the Comments made by the author and the Collaborators of the documents

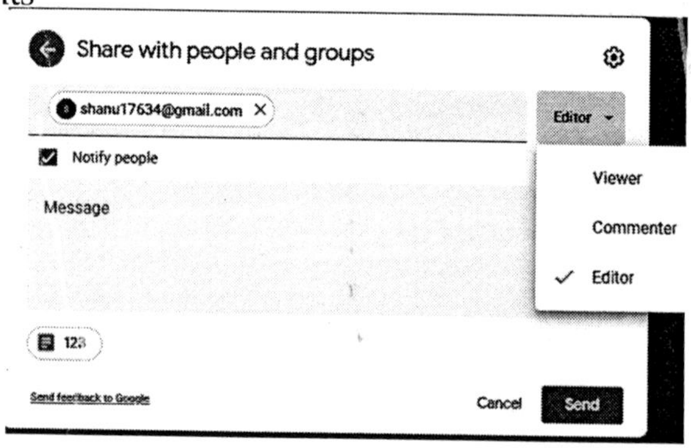

Share Button : this helps to share the document with other collaborators; an author can allow the collaborator to either view it, comment on it, or edit. The author can also include a message while sharing the document. The selected collaborator will be notified, and the document will be shared via Google drive.

Format Tab of the Google Doc : Doc has a very handy format bar. It also has an editing button in the right-hand top corner to edit, suggest or view the document.

In the sidebar of the Google doc, there are shortcuts to Google Calendar; Google Keep; and Google Tasks.

Google Docs is a useful tool for creating, editing, saving, and collaborating documents. Two or more people can work on a document at same the time, so it allows real-time collaboration. Its full version with all its features can be freely accessed from any browser. As everything is automatically saved in Google drive, so no loss of data in case of power-off or accidentally close out of the programme.

GOOGLE SLIDES

Google Slides is a web-based free presentation programme provided by Google since 2006, which can be used to create, edit, and collaborate with others to make professional presentations and present wherever you are. Google Slides is an incredibly versatile tool.

STEPS TO CREATE A NEW GOOGLE SLIDE

1. Log in to https://docs.google.com/presentation/u/0/
2. Click on + sign (Blank).
3. By default, the document name of the document will be "Untitled presentation". Click on it and give a name

STEPS TO UPLOAD A DOCUMENT

1. User can upload a document from his computer (the format supported are.ppt; .pptx and .pps.
2. Go to Google Drive, click on new >file upload>go to the location of the file to be uploaded>select the file>open; alternatively, open a new presentation click on open and browse and upload from the computer.

Once a new presentation in Google Slides is created, an interface displaying the main menu will appear. This facilitates users to create and modify slides, select themes as per choice, and add collaborators to the presentation and finally present (Ctrl+Shift+F5).

Theme of Google Slide : The first step of making the presentation is to choose the appropriate theme i.e. design of the presentation. "A theme is a preset group of colors, fonts, backgrounds, and layouts." By default, about 30 themes are provided by Google but one can import themes from other websites also. The theme controls the impression of the presentation, presenter leaves it in the minds of the viewers. Choosing an appropriate theme is very important, they should reflect the ideas of the presentation, try to use a simple theme with fewer colours as the content is more important, a theme should not supersede the main idea of the presentation.

Layout : Layout is the arrangement (Font, colour, position, etc.) of text and images on a slide. To change the layout of the slide, select it, click Layout, and choose the layout as per the requirement of the slide.

Background: Background is the picture or color behind the slide's content. To change the background, click on the 'Background' from the toolbar, choose the colour, choose the image. You can also add his background as a new theme.

Adding, Removing, and Hiding Slides : It is very easy

to add a new blank slide, even an identical one to the existing slide or to delete a slide or even hide a slide during the presentation. Right-click the slide thumbnail of the exiting slide and choose either new' or 'Duplicate' or 'Delete' or 'Skip Slide' respectively. Once a slide is hidden the slide will fade and will not the part of the show. You can un-hide it by unchecking the 'Skip Slide'.

MENU BAR OF GOOGLE SLIDE

The interface has a typical menu containing commands grouped by function and the shortcut toolbar has buttons of commands which are frequently used.

File : This button is the same as Google Docs having the basic "sharing, editing and toggling settings".

Edit : Edit tab has the normal editing and formatting button like other Google programmes: Google docs and Google sheets.

View : The View tab is for the screen set up and set up the show.

- Present (Ctrl +F5) lets one make the presentation;
- Motion (Ctrl+Alt+Shift+B) is for setting the animation and transition of the slide. One can choose the type of animation of the object and transition of the slide, from the pop-up window opened on clicking on the motion;
- Master opens the slide master for the document. It helps to choose the predefined layouts for the presentation;
- The grid view shows all the slides of the presentations by grid formation. In this view, one can reorder slides by dragging. To close the Grid view, go to the View tab and un-tick it;
- Zoom and ruler work the same as any office management programmes;
- Guides help to add guidelines to the presentation, vertical/horizontal guide can be added. These lines help

to place text and objects in the presentation;

Snap to can be used to align objects on a slide automatically:

- Snap to Guides : When an object is dragged, coloured lines appear, these lines show the center of the slide;
- Snap to Grid : When an object is dragged, it aligns to an invisible grid on the slide.
- Show Speaker notes: by clicking on it speakers notes can be seen under the slides
- Fullscreen can be used to see the slides on fullscreen

Insert: An image, Text box, Audio, Video, Shape, Table, Chart, Word art, diagram, Line, Special Character, Animation, Link (Ctrl+K), Comment (Ctrl+Alt+M), New Slide(Ctrl +M), Slide numbers, and Pace holder can be added to a slide using Insert tab;

Format: Format tab used to customize the slide text. Size, Colour, Capitalisation, and more settings can be done. Text aligns can be aligned; numbering and bullets can be added; Borders and lines can be created and edit a border;

Slide : Slide can be used to add, duplicate, skip, and remove slides from the presentation. It can be used to move the 'slide' option to change the order of the slides. Change of background, layout, animation, theme, and transition of the Slide can be done using this tab.

Slide Master : Slide master is used to creating a Master Slide and Master Layout. The master slide is a presentation template that consists of all the elements which one wants to include in his every presentation, maybe the logo or specific background, color, fonts, effects, etc. The master layout is preparing a default layout by using a combination of placeholder and graphics which can be used for one or more slides of the presentation. These are editable and if changes are made to the "master", changes are applied automatically to every slide of the presentation. This saves a lot of time. To create a slide master, click on the Slide Menu, select Edit Master, and make the changes in Master and layouts and rename it. When finished, quit by clicking the small x on the right corner.

Arrange : The Arrange tab has all the alignment tools:

- **Order :** Order can be used to bring to front or forward or send to back or backward any object in the slide;
- **Align :** Alignhelps to align the objects on the slide at right, left, or center;
- **Distribute :** This option allows distributing the vertical and horizontal spacing between the selected elements evenly;
- **Center on page :** This option will help to arrange the object vertically/horizontally centered on the current slide;
- **Rotate :** This option helps to rotate the object clockwise or anti-clockwise or to flip it horizontally or vertically;
- **Group and Ungroup :** Grouping can be for the objects (shape, textbox, bar chart, etc.). Grouped items stay together when moved or resized. To group the objects first, select all the objects that are to be grouped, then click on arrange and then group (alternatively right-click the selected objects and then click group or press Ctrl+Alt+ G. To ungroup the objects, select the group, then click on arrange and then group (alternatively right-click > Ungroup or Ctrl+Alt+Shift+G).

Add-ons : Google Slide is a very powerful tool for everyone who wants to make a presentation. It has almost all features of Microsoft Power-Point Add-ons makes it more powerful than Microsoft Power-point. Add-ons can be installed by clicking on the Add-ons tab from the menu bar and choosing the Add-on and then installing it. A list of some of the add-ons which can be used with the slides is given below:

- **Equation Editor++ :** This add-on is used to put equations in the slide with the power of LaTeX and the simplicity of a graphical editor. It can also be used with Google Docs.

- **Icons from Flaticon :** This Add-on gives access to a large database of Icons and can be used with Google Docs, Google Slides, Google Spreadsheets, and Google Forms.
- **Icons from Noun Project :** This Add-on enables the adding of icons directly to the presentations without ever leaving Google Slides. Icons are used to visually illustrate any idea. The add-on provides access to 1 million royalty-free icons;
- **Images, Gifs, and more :** This Add-on can be used with Google docs and sheets and slides to add royalty-free Images, Gifs, Icons, Stickers, Emojis, and Illustrations to the document.
- **Insert Icons :** Insert Icons is also available for Google Sheets and Docs, it can be used to various icons to the slides which can be further formatted. Around 1,800 icons are available in every color and can be inserted into the slides.
- **LucidChart Diagrams :** This can be used to create Flowcharts, Mind maps, Venn diagrams, Wireframes, and mockups right into their presentations, no exporting is required.
- **Magic Rainbow Unicorn :** This Add-on can be used to add rainbow colors to all of the text without needing to individually change each letter;
- **Nearpod :** Nearpod helps teachers to engage students in the classroom via virtual reality, 3D objects, PhET simulations, etc. It can also incorporate open-ended questions, polls, quizzes, collaborative boards, gamified activities, etc.
- **Paletti :** Paletti can be used to colour the slides at the click of a button. You can even extract a colour palette from a selected image. Around 200 palettes are preloaded and

ready for use.

- **PearDeck :** PearDeckcan is used to engage the audience with the help of interactive questions, polls, and formative assessments during the presentation itself.
- **ScriptSlide :** ScriptSlide is a Google Slides add-on that takes the speaker notes in the Google Slides and displays them in a teleprompter-like screen that the speaker can control with the smartphone;
- **Slide Randomizer :** Slide Randomizer is a simple add-on that allows one to easily and randomly reorder any slide deck.
- **Slides Background :** This Add-on helps to generate beautiful material backgrounds for the presentations with 16 different color themes;
- **Slides Toolbox :** This is a very helpful add-on to install. It cuts the clicks on repeated tasks and brings features for organizing and unifying data in Google Slides. It can be used as a Remove tool, text tool, arrangement tool, Export-Import Tool, Chart/Image/Object tool, Page tool, etc.
- **Unsplash :** Unsplash add-on gives access to hundreds of thousands of HD photos (copyright free, personal, and commercial) which can be added to the presentation.
- **Help :** The help menu can be used to get help for using the slides, get training to use slides, get the update, send feedback, Report abuse/copyright, see the Privacy Policy and terms and conditions to use slides. Keyboard shortcuts can also be accessed from this menu.
- **Comments History Button :** This tells about the Comments made by the author and the Collaborators of the documents
- **Present :** If a presentation is to be made press the Present button on the menu bar, a full-screen presentation will appear, to exit full-screen, press the Esc key.

- **Share :** Share Button like other Google programmes like sheet doc or forms helps to share the document via Google drive with other collaborators.

Google slide is powerful presentation software and it is very user-friendly. It's Google's equivalent to Microsoft PowerPoint or Apple's Keynote; it's in the cloud, it is super easy to use and most importantly, it's free and can be worked in collaboration. Many features have been added over the past few years and Google is continuously updating it.

REFERENCES

My Apps Georgia Southern University Learning Center (2020). What are Google Apps? https://sites.google.com/a/georgiasouthern.edu/google-apps-fac-staff/getting-started/why-google

https://blog.hubspot.com/marketing/google-docs-tips

https://www.brightcarbon.com/blog/google-slides-ultimate-guide/

7

Google Sheets

For Teaching and Learning

Google Sheets or a worksheet is a file made in a tabular format consisting of rows and columns, for visualizing, calculating, and organizing the data. It is a free, web-based spreadsheet program provided by Google since 2014 and it is almost similar to the Microsoft Excel programme. Google Sheets is a convenient method for real-time collaboration, compilation, sharing, reviewing, and presentation of data and information. It can do complex analysis and can handle 2 million data sets. It is very easy to use and various readymade templates are available and support about 83 languages. The major benefit of using Google Sheets is, one can edit and share their spreadsheet files over the internet making them useful for all kinds of tasks. Many third-party add-ons enhance the usability and functionality of Google Spreadsheets. Google sheet gives the facility to create their dashboards; write formulas use of built-in applications to automate any job.

STEPS TO CREATE A NEW GOOGLE SPREADSHEET

1. Log in to sheets.google.com
2. Click on + sign (Blank).
3. By default, the document name of the document will be "Untitledspreadsheet". Click on it and give a name

STEPS TO UPLOAD A DOCUMENT

1. User can upload a document from his computer (format supported are.xls and .xlsx; .ods; .csv and .tsv; .txt; .tsb) into Google spreadsheet format.
2. Go to Google Drive, click on new >file upload>go to the location of file to be uploaded>select the file>open; alternatively, open a new spreadsheet click on open and browse and upload from the computer.

FILL THE DATA IN THE SPREADSHEET

1. User can type the data by clicking on each cell;
2. User can copy and paste from another spreadsheet;
3. User can copy an HTML table from a website;
4. Users can import an existing spreadsheet or excel sheet.

DRAGGING 'DATA' IN A SPREADSHEET

1. Dragging is an important feature of a spreadsheet. It helps to either copy the same number or formula across all the cells where dragging is done or to continue the number.
2. If a user wants to select the data or formula, click on the cell, and from the bottom-right corner of a highlighted cell pull down the cursor across or down a range of cells.
3. If a user wants to do some numbering, write numbers on two cells, select both the cells, and drag.

BASIC TERMINOLOGY

Cell : A sheet is a grid of cells. "a cell is a rectangular box that occurs at the intersection of a vertical column and a horizontal row in a sheet", it holds the actual data of the sheet.

Columns : Columns runs vertically in the grid layout of a sheet, they are labeled by letters (A, B, C....) running across the top of the Sheet.

Rows : Rows run horizontally in the grid layout of a sheet, labeled by numbers (1,2,3…..) running down the left side of the Sheet.

Cell Reference/Address : A Cell Reference/ Address is an alphanumeric value (letter for column and number for rows) used to identify a specific cell in a spreadsheet. For example- First column, First row: A1 or Twentieth column and Twenty-Third row: AB23

Range : Range is a selection of cells extending across a row, column, or both.

Spreadsheet : The entire document containing your worksheets

MENU BAR OF GOOGLE SPREADSHEET

File Edit View Insert Format Slide Arrange Tools Add-ons Help Accessibility Last edit was seconds ago

File

The File menu has items that deal with the document as a whole

- Share, New, Open, Make a copy, Email, Make available Offline, Version history, Rename, Moveare same, Add shortcut to the drive, Move to trash, Publish to the Web, Document details and print are same as Google Doc.
- Import is importing data from another sheet and creating a new sheet with that data;

Download

A user can download the sheet at his device in one of the following formats:

- Microsoft Excel (.xlxs)
- OpenDocument Format (.ods)
- PDF Document (.pdf)
- Web Page (.html, zipped)
- Comma-separated values (.csv, current sheet)

- Tab-separated values (.tsv, current sheet)

Spreadsheet settings : here the size and the orientation of the sheet can be set.

Edit Menu

Edit Menu has some regular options like 'undo' (ctrl+z); 'redo' (ctrl+y); 'cut' (ctrl+x); 'copy' (ctrl+c); 'paste' (ctrl+v); 'find and replace' (ctrl+h)

Paste Special : This option has a choice in pasting the selected data. Options available are- Paste values only; Paste format only; Paste all except borders; Paste formula only; Paste data validation only; Paste conditional formatting only; Paste transpose (Pastes a rotated version of the copied cells.)

- Other options in the Edit menu are: Delete Values; Delete row 1; Delete Column A; Delete cells and Shift up; Delete cells and Shift left; and Clear notes

View Menu

Freeze : The sheet has option of Freezing any column or row of the active sheet. It will help in keeping the selected row or column visible even in the case of scrolling down or right.

Gridlines : This feature shows the gridlines of the sheet, if unchecked the gridlines will disappear.

Protected Ranges : If the creator/editor has marked some cells or sheets as protected, by clicking on the 'Protected Ranges' those cells and sheets will be highlighted.

Formula Bar : By clicking on 'Formula bar the *fx* menu of the formula will appear under the editing pan.

Show Formula : It will show the formula applied for the calculations

- Hidden Sheet (to display the hidden sheet of the document); Zoom and Fullscreen are the other options available on the View menu bar

Insert Menu

This menu is for inserting Row above, Row below, column left, column right, cells and shift down, cells and shift right, chart, and image (image can be taken from the drive or any connected devices covering has the option of 'Image in Cell' or Image over Cells'), drawing, Google form.

- Functions/formulas can also be added to the sheet for calculations. Normal functions like SUM, AVERAGE, COUNT, MAX, and MIN are inbuilt in the Sheet. There are about 500 functions that are incorporated with the sheet and categorized into subjects like Engineering, Mathematics, Statistical, etc. A user can use a customized formula to do the calculations. For adding a formula start with the '=' sign before inputting a formula. Now input the formula for the calculation without any gap, press enter;
- Insert a link (ctrl+k), checkbox, comment (ctrl+alt+m), Note (Shift+F2), and New Sheet (Shit+F11) are the other commands in the Insert Menu.

Format Menu

The format menu of the spreadsheet is to format the cells, columns, rows, worksheets, and the workbook. This menu also gives users access to templates of standard formats.

- Standard, simple Light, streamline, paradigm, Shift, etc are the available themes to change the looks of the sheets.
- Number pan gives the option to format numbers, dates, and currencies, to format the data of a cell or range of cells, select the data to be formatted, and click on the number in the format menu. Select an option from the list, the format will be applied to the selected cells.
- Other options like Bold, Italic Underline, Strikethrough, Font size, Align, Merge Cells, Text Wrapping, Text rotation, alternating colors, and clear formatting are available in the Format Menu.

- Conditional Formatting can be set for the specific cells. Click the Conditional formatting in the Format menu, A toolbar will open to the right, create a rule under "Format cells if", choose the condition that you want to trigger the rule, and click on done

Data Menu

In the data menu of the spreadsheet various utilities are provided to alter and format data.

Sorting Data : Data can be sorted from highest to lowest or lowest to highest or in alphabetical order also range-wise. For sorting, highlight the area 'this is to be sorted', including the header row. Then from the menu: Data > Sort range..., you can select the column option from A to Z or Z to A. This re-sorts the table, showing the earliest members first.

Filtering Data : Data can be filtered in the spreadsheet by hiding some of the values and only data relevant to the problem will be displayed. To filter data click on a cell containing data in the table, and then click Filter from the Data menu, the selected data will be highlighted and have a border, now click on create a filter. Now give the name of the filter and rage of data for applying the filter. Click the little green triangle next to the column heading on which filter has to be applied, it will open the filter menu. Data can be filtered by colour, condition (is empty; not empty, text content, the text does not contain, texts start with, texts ends with, the text is exactly, Date is, the date is before, the date is after, Greater than, Greater than and equal to, less than, less than and equal to, is equal to, is not equal to, is between, is not between or any customized formula) and values. Now we can have the filter view and the normal view also. The filter can be removed by clicking on the triangle button again or under the "Filter by conditions" set the rule to "None".

Slicers : Slicers is a new feature added to the spreadsheet, they can be used to filter data in Pivot Tables. They make it easy to change values in Pivot Tables and Charts with a single click. To add a slicer to a chart or pivot table, click on it>Data>Slicer. A pop-up will appear in the right-hand side corner, choose a column to filter by, click the slicer, and choose the filter rules.

Data Validation : Data Validation is a feature that's most commonly used to add dropdown lists into cells within Sheets. Go to Data > Data Validation and select from several options under "Criteria." It can be used for many things like by choosing the "dates" option in data validation we can Track upcoming work; to automatically mark the checkbox with a value; to protect structured data we can 'Reject input' for invalid entries.

Pivot Table : Pivot table helps to analyze a large amount of data by summarizing it. To use this feature, select the cells with data that is to be summarized then click on Data>Pivot table. This will create a new tab in the Sheet called "Pivot Table 1" with the Pivot Table framework in place. Set the criteria for rows, columns, values, and filters and click apply.

Randomize Range : Randomize range is used to sort the selected range in random order. Select the list of data that has to be sort randomly, and then right-click, then choose Randomize range from the context menu.

Named Ranges : We can give a name to one or more cells or a formula, it will help us to easily reuse, recall, and read that have been given a name. They also provide simple navigation via the Name Box. To use Names ranges select the cells which are to be renamed>Data>Named ranges. A menu will open on the right. Type the range name of your choice.

Protected Sheets and ranges : If a user wants his content of the spreadsheet is not changed by anyone, the data can be protected. The spreadsheet can be printed, copied and import and export copies will be possible but data will be static. To protect a sheet or a range click on Protected sheets and ranges from the data menu, a pop-up will appear, add a sheet or range (to protect a range, one needs to click on Range, and to protect a sheet one has to click on Sheet), set permissions, click on Save or Done.

Spit text to columns : By using this option a user can split clearly defined data (text separated by commas, periods, or spaces) into several columns. If the data is already in the spreadsheet, select the data to go to the Data menu and click on the Split text to columns. If data is at some other place, paste it into a column. A pop-up will appear in the lower right-hand corner of the data. Click on it, and an option to split the data into columns will appear.

Remove Duplicates : Sometimes our data in the spreadsheet may have some duplicate entries, the same record may be appearing more than once. To remove such kind of data Remove duplicate option can be used. Click on the option from the Data menu, a pop-up will appear asking which columns or rows are to be checked for duplicates, select the rows or columns and click on remove duplicates.

Trim whitespaces : This option is to remove additional white spaces from the sheet, leaving just a single space between words. To do so select the range, column or rows, click on trim whitespaces from the data menu and click ok.

Group and ungroup : There is a provision of grouping in Google Sheets for specific rows and columns even different worksheets and shapes which have a similar type of data. The advantage of grouping is whatever action is taken applies to every item of the group. To group, select the items which are to be brought together then go to Group in the data menu (or alt+shit+'!), and to ungroup select the items which are to be ungrouped than go to Ungroup in the data menu (or alt+shit+!)

Tools Menu

Tool menu is to facilitate the functioning of the spreadsheet.

Create a form : This is similar to the insert Google form option and it will automatically be linked to a new sheet that's created within the spreadsheet;

Script Editor : Script editor is for the programmers and person who knows how to write the code can use this option;

Macros : Macros are a set of stored functions that can be used in a spreadsheet to automate processes that are repeated often. A user can create and record Macro, manage a macro, and even import a macro from a different sheet. To record a macro click on record macro from the tools menu, a pop-up saying regarding a macro will be there on the screen, make the changes you want to see, and save the macro with a name, number is optional. Next time when you want to use any saved macro go to the macros tool menu and select the macro you want to use.

Spelling : Spell check functions just as the other spell checks and all the other Google products to check the spelling and grammar;

Enable Autocomplete : One can turn on or off this feature. This feature helps to predict the next letter as you're typing based on what you've previously typed;

Notification Rules : Enabling this feature, the author of the sheet is notified through Gmail if any changes are made to the form or if any user submits a form. Settings can be done about notifying immediately or once in a week

Protect Sheet : This feature helps to protect the sheet or a range. User can give that a name and then set the permissions about who can make any changes to it;

- Accessibility settings are the same as Google Docs.

Add-ons

Originally Google apps were considered very simpler and less powerful alternatives to Microsoft Office. But over time, Google relentlessly added features to make up the difference and it added Add-ons to each of their apps in 2014. There are about 250 add-ons that can be added to Google. To add these add-ons to Google Sheets, go to the add-ons menu in the top right, and click get add-ons. This will open the Sheets Add-ons store, where one can search through over or sort them by category. Then click the free button that appears, and accept the permissions. Now the add-on is ready to use. Some of the Popular add-ons are:

Advanced Find & Replace : This add-on searches and replaces the values, formulas, notes, and hyperlinks of all the Google Sheets at once.

Advanced Summary : This add-on can be used to quickly build a summary of the form responses;

Autocrat : This is a multi-purpose document merge tool used to automate the creation and sharing of personalized documents by taking data from a spreadsheet and merge it into a document via a template;

CopyDown : CopyDown helps to add formulas to form responses.

Doctopus : Doctopus gives teachers the ability to mass-copy, share, monitor student progress, and manage grading and feedback for student projects in Google Drive.

Flubaroo : This add-on helps educators grade and analyze online assignments and assessments quickly, as well as share scores with students;

Google Analytics : This is data management add-ons, it smoothens the process of managing, accessing, sharing, and visualizing the data in sheets much easier and streamlined manner;

Hunter : This add-on helps to find email addresses directly inside the spreadsheets;

Mail Merge : This add-on personalizes emails, letters, and envelopes by merging data from a Google Sheet;

Power Tools : This add-on cuts the clicks on repeated tasks and enhances the Google Sheets with features that organize and unify the data.

RowCall : This add-on sort rows from your main sheet by the column you select and creates individual sheets for every unique cell in that column;

Save As Doc : This add-on can be used to convert the Google Sheets into a Google Document;

Supermetrics : This add-on is a sidebar that allows user to pull the metrics and dimensions directly into the selected cells;

Table Styles : This add-on helps to apply a professional and uniform look to the tables in Google Sheets;

Template Gallery for Sheets : This add-on helps add templates to the spreadsheet;

Translate My Sheet : This add-on helps to translate the spreadsheet in more than 100 languages;

Tweet Archiver : The Twitter Archiver lets the user easily save tweets for any search keyword or hashtag in a Google Spreadsheet;

XLMiner Analysis ToolPak : This add-on can be used for statistical analyses;

Yet Another Mail Merge : This is a mail merge tool for Gmail. Send mass emails with high deliverability directly from Google Sheets and Gmail

Help

Help menu can be used to search the menu (alt+/); look for the help regarding use of sheet; look for updates; send feedback regarding some issue; Abuse and copyright issues can be reported; look for the privacy policy regarding the use of sheet and terms of use of the sheet. It also has a list of functions that can be used in sheets and keyboard shortcuts.

Toolbar in the spreadsheet

The spreadsheet toolbar displays many shortcuts to spreadsheet menu items and actions. These buttons provide direct access to particular operations. One can customize the buttons that appear on the toolbar using the Tools>Customize Toolbar menu.

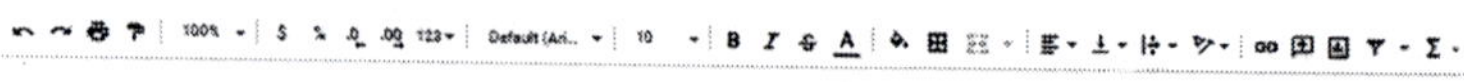

Adding worksheets in Google sheets : The bottom of the window lists the number of sheets of the document, by clicking the + will add a new sheet.

Collaboration : Collaborative working on Google sheet is just like Google docs by using the share button;

- The comment history button provides notifications and comments by collaborators.
- Sidebar provides access to Google Calendar, Keep, and Tasks.

Google sheets can be used to perform mathematical calculations on statistical data. It can be used for totaling long columns of numbers or determining percentages and averages. Integration of several third-party add-ons and the ability to work in collaboration make it better than Microsoft Excel.

8

YouTube

Educating the Generations

The sharing of videos is quite challenging and the young and innovative people are interested to share their creativity in such a platform which may allow any user irrespective of their religion, place, and another dynamics of the physical and digital environment. There are several video sharing applications are available in the market. Twitch, Vimeo, Swarmify, Veoh, Dailymotion, and Metacafe are some popular video sharing application tools but YouTube is most acceptable due to the user-friendly platform and powered by Google. Due to Google, it is now a more powerful platform to be used as a showcase for creativity and entertainment. Alexa service is analyzing YouTube and other such online services on the internet and according to Alexa, YouTube is the third largest online service viewed every month by the users and second after Wikipedia in engaging the internet traffic (Alexa, n.d.). YouTube is one step ahead of its competitors because it is merely not a video-sharing application but also it encourages to production, edit, submit and sharing of video content in such a manner where a kid or young or older generation may bring their videos. After observing the impact and importance of social media, the University Grants Commission suggested to all HEIs (Higher Educational Institutes) to appoint 'Social

Media Champions' in their institutions. The Social Media Champions may upload the activities of the students and teachers, lectures, and other academic work over social media platforms such as FACEBOOK, WHATSAPP, INSTAGRAM, and YOUTUBE, etc. The YOUTUBE Chanel has to be created by the institutions to reach every student/ faculty member and other members of the institution. Millions of YouTube Channels are there to extend the needs of academic learning through their live and recorded videos. 'TED-Ed' is one of the best education channel *(https://www.youtube.com/user/TEDEducation/videos)* where educators and animators work in collaboration to share knowledge on various innovations. In the field of aeronautics and space explosion, NASA has developed its YouTube channel *(https://www.youtube.com/user/NASAtelevision/videos)* which gives the latest development and research output in this field. They are uploading six videos in a day since 2008. 'MIT CourseWare' is one of the very popular YouTube channel (https://www.youtube.com/c/mitocw) created by the Massachusetts Institute of Technology (MIT), USA. It is making available contents of their materials used for their various open courses on science and technology. Likewise, Microsoft Education, minutephysics, Khan Academy, CrashCourse, Big think, T-Series Kids Hut, and Stanford University, etc. are some popular YouTube channels in the field of academic and research which are followed by a huge number of students and academicians throughout the world.

BACKGROUND

Jawed Karim, Steve Chen, and Chad Hurley developed an online video-sharing service in 2005. All these three gentlemen were working with PayPal online payment services. The headquarter of YouTube is situated in San Bruno, California. This American company was taken over by Google in November 2006. Now YouTube is one of the most promising parts of the Google application family (Phrasee, 2016).

YouTube is offering free services to all its customers with some advertisements which sometimes creates some disturbances in watching the videos of one's interest. Keeping in mind such problems, YouTube launched its the name 'YouTube Red' in 2014 But it has some problems still. With some modification, the YouTube Premium version is been launched under a very nominal monthly subscription price (Spangler, n.d.). The Premium version is free from any kind of commercials and advertisement and also available with music keys.

4Fs AND YOUTUBE

YouTube works with a mission 'to give everyone a voice and show them the world' ("YouTube," 2020). YouTube is taking care of not only the emotional aspects of one's life but also privacy and freedom. The person may express himself without any fear or any apprehension. Whereas, they may explore their creativity and present it to the world with ease. YouTube describes that they are working with these basic objectives. They are:

(i) Freedom of Expression

(ii) Freedom of Information

(iii) Freedom of Opportunity

(iv) Freedom to Belong

VARIOUS PRODUCTS

Initially, it was only YouTube but the demand and contents available on YouTube, they have arranged contents under various categories for ease of the viewers and YouTube lovers. They are as follows:

YouTube TV

YouTube has recently launched 'YouTube TV' which allows to access more than 85 channels. But they are available in the United States of America only. You need to use a zip code and service will be provided. It is a paid service and one account may be shared with six other contacts of the family without any extra charges. There is no need for DVR and setup boxes, unlike traditional TVs. The internet is the only requirement to use the YouTube TV service. It may work on any of the computing devices like mobile phones, computers, notebooks, laptops, etc. It may be accessed on *https://tv.youtube.com/welcome/.*

YouTube Music

YouTube Music is dedicated to the music lovers of the world. The music from almost 60 countries is covered under this platform in several languages which is the huge one. Even songs from more than 09 Indian Languages are available under this. The songs are available under PLAYLISTS, ALBUMS, SONGS, ARTISTS, and SUBSCRIPTIONS. The songs may be chosen according to the genre and mood too. Therefore, YouTube Music is a new revolution under the music category. Due to Google's support, it is one of the major searchable music platforms across the world.

YouTube Kids

YouTube Kids is one of the best services of YouTube. It is purely dedicated to the kids and their parents. The content on this platform is free from pornography and other unaccepted content for the kids. The best part of it is that the control is with the parents of the kids. Without the approval of the parents, contents will not be available to the kids. Even the account will be open in the name and by the parents. The contents available on it is very entertaining and useful and presented in a very simpler form. This is an amazing and learning and entertainment platform for kids with all security and control of parents. The timer may be set by the parents to watch for their kids. The objectionable or unwanted contents may be blocked also. It is a more family-oriented channel of YouTube.

Creator Academy

YouTube has launched the 'Creator Academy' to assist the YouTuber or YouTube Chanel host to enhance visibility and earnings. The online training is available to understand how to increase subscribers and other benefits. One can learn how to make available your YouTube channel on all platforms like laptops, TV Screens, mobiles, and games, etc (Hypebot, 2013). To be a part of YouTube Creator Academy, one must have more than 1000 subscribers, more than 4000 public watch hours in the last one year (12 Months), and an AdSense linked account.

YouTube for Artists

'YouTube for Artists' is dedicated to the artists where their creativity such as music videos, songs, albums, etc of many channels will come together automatically. It is known as 'Official Artist Channels (OAC)'. The OAC offers three basic services to the artists ("YouTube," 2020):

Organized content : The Official Artist Channel layout automatically organizes your discography into an album section and your Official Music Videos into a new playlist. You have the option to move, delete, and re-add either of these auto-generated music sections from your channel.

Promotional content : Promotional content allows a YouTuber to choose what he wants to highlight in the featured video slot. The description of the video should be crisp, small, and to the point. It helps to attract the audience. The video should compliance with be ADSENSE Google.

Fan engagement : One verified and official channel where you can directly reach and interact with your fans on YouTube.

There are some mandatory and some optional criteria to create their own 'Official Artist Channel'. YouTube allows creating an OAC to an artist if he/she qualifies followings-

The Mandatory Criteria:

- Own and operate a YouTube channel that represents one artist or band
- Have at least 3 official releases on YouTube delivered and distributed by a music distributor or label
- Have no policy violations on your channel

The optional Criteria (At least one should be there):

- Work with a YouTube Partner Manager
- Be part of the YouTube Partner Program
- Your channel is part of a label network that works with a Partner Manager

FEATURES

YouTube has gained popularity and a special space among every age group because of its user-friendly features. Most importantly, they are dedicated and developed in light of social media generations. Some of the attractive features are:

Trending : Under this category, YouTube brings and suggest you the most views or popular videos to the user. It also matches with your past searchers and automatically provides you the most viewed videos of your choice.

Subscriptions : Subscriptions are one of the best features of YouTube. The content you liked under some YouTube channel and wants to see again or any content which is going to upload in the future. In such a case, you have to subscribe to the channel and whenever the content will be uploaded on the same, one will be intimated automatically and enjoy the same. The earnings and popularity of the channel are also based on subscriptions/subscribers of the particular channel.

Library : Under Library, every activity of the viewer is saved automatically. The library is the collection of activities such as history, downloads, videos, your movies, and 'Watch Later'. The saved and downloaded videos for offline use is available under this one. One can download the video if that channel is allowing it. It is very useful while you want to see content offline.

History : The history feature is the total count and details of your watched activity on YouTube. You can manage history by various types too. You can clear browsed history and even you can pause your watched history. Once you clear your watched history, you will not be able to recall your past activity. You can search for any video content through any keyword or combination of keywords under the default 'Search Box'. Your search pattern leads to create a list of videos of interest which is automatically created by YouTube. While you open YouTube, you will see the videos related to your past searches. Sometimes these are very useful and sometimes they are irritating too. In this way, it is suggested to remove your search history also to get fresh videos on other subjects.

Your videos : Your videos will show you the videos uploaded by you on various channels. In a single click, you can see all your uploaded content on YouTube. It is a very good option for YouTubers.

Watch later : 'Watch later' is one of the activities where the viewer may save video content to see later when you find the time. It is like to make selections of the videos and bookmark them for future use.

Liked videos : It is one of the options where a viewer may see all his liked videos. The 'Liked Videos' is one of the features used by YouTube too to rate particular videos. It is useful for the viewer that all liked videos may be arranged at the same place. If by mistake you liked some video content on YouTube, you can also revert it.

Explore : Explore is the trigger to watch videos under various interesting eight categories. These categories are Trending, Music, Gaming, News, Films, Fashion & Beauty, Learning, and Live. The 'Live' category is one of the great resources under YouTube. One can join the live broadcasting programmes under this segment.

CREATING A CHANNEL

Creating a channel on YouTube is very important to showcase your creativity. For public presence, you need to have a channel on YouTube to upload content (videos), comments, rates, and reviews. There are two types of channels are created on YouTube i.e. Personal and Business. In both cases, one must have a Gmail account. The Business account is known as Brand Accounts. To create the Brand Account, one has to select 'Your Chanel List' and under it, the Brand account may be created. The photograph/logo of the brand may be used under this category. Repetition of the channel is not allowed under this category i.e. if you have already a channel under this, you can not create another one.

UPLOADING VIDEOS

To upload the video, one has to first sign-in on YouTube through his/her Gmail account. At the top right, one can find a 'plus (+) Create' option. Under this, one is for 'upload videos' and another is 'Go Live'. 'Go live' is used for live streaming. Under live streaming videos may be obtained from any suitable broadcasting or video conferencing software like Zoom, WebEx and Streamyard, etc. Any other event may also make live through YouTube too but this is not available with the free version of YouTube.

Videos may be uploaded on YouTube under the Brand account and individual channel. The video file format should be Mp4. All the descriptions about the content and banner may also be included in the video. YouTube also gives you all rights to make a video private or public. It is strictly asking for safety for kids or not. Under the setting option, all details must be filled in carefully.

CREATING PLAYLIST

'Playlist' is used to save videos on a similar subject or genre. It is very simple to create your playlist. Simply, open the video on youtube and choose the option 'save+' and you can save the video on the pre-defined Playlist or you can create a new one. For example, your interest area is Digital Library. You can create a playlist with the name 'Digital Library' and all the videos related to the same may be saved under this playlist.

YOUTUBE FOR LIBRARIES

YouTube is one of the best media to interact with the students, researchers, and faculty members. The libraries may use YouTube to showcasing their services and information products. The training and awareness drive on information resources, research techniques, and other activities may be executed. Dr. Preeti Sharda, Librarian PGGDC-42, Chandigarh has created a channel 'Friday Fables: Stories' on youtube where stories reading activity is been done by various storytellers.

'Open Library Foundation' is one of the channel to enable the access to open source and open access projects which is made for libraries and by the libraries. It was started in 2016 at Boaston. It first created an YouTube chanel for FOLIO programme where the interviews of conference was made availbe. It may be accessed through *https://www.youtube.com/channel/UC4Vs5mb1qgOXPZgso1LESUw.*

National Digital Library of India (NDLI) has created its own YouTube Chanel *(https://www.youtube.com/watch?v=mF8xIAN3Dxo)* to aware the students and teachers right from primary to post graduate level about the contents availbe on NDLI. Under NDLI, millions of educational video contents are availbe to access and share for learning and research.

The book reviews and other information dissemination may be done using YouTube by creating channels by the libraries. The virtual tour guide of the library, small training and search and research strategy may be created for their users in particular and others too. Therefore, YouTube is one of the very powerful ICT tools for libraries in promoting education and research.

CONCLUSION

Express your creativity with honesty and integrity is one of the motives of YouTube. It is a free and affordable service of Google to entertain, educate, and showcasing the creativity of individuals and groups. Its reach is from the dense modern city to the most remotely situated village. It needs nothing but an internet connection to experience the wave of YouTube. It is like a revolution for every genre of age and society. It gives complete analytics of your videos too. For example, you can see how many comments you get on your videos or how many liked your videos, or how many hours it has been seen by the viewers.

Learning and earning is another feature of it. Your creativity may respond to you with earnings on YouTube. In general, search and related video recommendation persistently drive steady views to a video (Zhou et al., 2016). The education sector is hugely benefitted from YouTube. The solution to everything is now available on YouTube. Libraries are also creating their channels to extend their research services for the promotion of education and research among the students, teachers, and academicians.

REFERENCES:

Alexa. (n.d.). *youtube.com Competitive Analysis, Marketing Mix and Traffic – Alexa.* Retrieved November 23, 2020, from https://www.alexa.com/siteinfo/youtube.com

Hypebot. (2013, May 22). Google Launches Free YouTube Creator Academy Courses To Maximize Your Channel. *Hypebot.* https://www.hypebot.com/hypebot/2013/05/google-launches-free-youtube-creator-academy-courses-to-maximize-your-channel.html

Phrasee. (2016, May 9). *The history of YouTube.* Phrasee. https://phrasee.co/the-history-of-youtube/

Spangler, T. (n.d.). *YouTube Red Launches: Is It Really Worth $10 per Month? - Variety.* Retrieved November 23, 2020, from https://variety.com/

2015/digital/news/youtube-red-launches-10-per-month-1201629071/

YouTube. (2020). In *Wikipedia*. https://en.wikipedia.org/w/index.php?title=YouTube&oldid=989612311

Zhou, R., Khemmarat, S., Gao, L., Wan, J., & Zhang, J. (2016). How YouTube videos are discovered and its impact on video views. *Multimedia Tools and Applications, 75*. https://doi.org/10.1007/s11042-015-3206-0

9

Google Site

Express Yourself

Public exposure is one of the reasons to choose or create a website for your creativity or work/business. World Wide Web (W3) is the landmark event created at CERN by Tim Berners-Lee, a British scientist in 1989(CERN, 2020) the entire technology of communication over the internet is based on hypertext. The purpose was to present something to the public which is not known to them. In that way, WWW started its journey. The first website (Nix, 2020) of CERN was launched on 06th August 1991 by Time Berners with the URL-http://info.cern.ch. Since then, now almost everyone whether individual or business or charity having their website to showcase their products and productivity and at the same time to attract them towards their work. Therefore, the website is one of the modern days' tools to interact, communicate and exchange views, products and marketing of services. Educational institutions are attracting students and their parents through their attractive websites. Because websites are one of the major and important tools of information dissemination. There are two types of websites are available:

I. Static : "A static website contains Web pages with fixed content. Each page is coded in HTML and displays the same information to every visitor. Static sites are the most basic type of website and are the easiest to create. Unlike dynamic websites, they do not require any Web programming or database design. A static site can be built by simply creating a few HTML pages and publishing them to a Web server" (TechTerms, 2020). Websites on forms, newsletter contents and documentation, etc. are some of the examples of the static type website.

II. Dynamic : "A dynamic website is a site that contains dynamic pages such as templates, contents, scripts, etc. In a nutshell, the dynamic website displays various content types every time it is browsed. The web page can be changed with the reader that opens the page, character of consumer interplay, or day time" (MonsterPost, 2020). To develop a dynamic website, the knowledge of coding languages and expertise is required.

One more aspect is also very important to understand the difference between a domain name and the name of the website and web address. Let me give you one example the URL of Dr. Ram Manohar Lohiya National Law University is *www.rmlnlu.ac.in*. Here first part 'rmlnlu' is the name of the website and the second part- '.ac.in' is the domain name. A domain name is denoting that the particular website belongs to which type of activity and country as well. Some of the popular domain name family are (WPBeginner, 2019)-

- .ac.in – for academic and Indian (www.rmlnlu.ac.in)
- .net – for networking (https://www.netcrackers.net)
- .org – for organization (www.archive.org)
- .com – for commercial (www.google.com)
- .edu – for educational (www.academia.edu)
- .CN – For China
- .UK – for the United Kingdom

ADVANTAGES OF HAVING A WEBSITE:

The Parachute (Parachute, n.d.) discussed a lot of advantages of having a website of your resources or work. Everyone must have some reasons to design and development of a website. There are some very pinpointed advantages of developing a website-

1. 24x7 visibility : It gives you to be available for your clients/users beyond the routine time limit. They can access your resources from any place any time round the clock. It means that a website assists you to be available all over the internet.

2. Credibility : The modern generation is more tech-savvy and would like to rate an institution/ business company through its presence in the online world. The users/customers always look forward to checking that whether that company/ institution is having a website, e-mail, and fax number. Because the website and their updated information make the company/institution credible. The more updated and more authentic information loaded website is deemed to achieve credibility in the market too.

3. Support and Service : Websites are one of the tools to provide support and services to their customers at any time. The problem of a customer/user may be resolved through online support and services. The websites are very useful in resolving the issues and getting more popularity among their users.

4. Market resistance : The access to the website round the clock and everywhere in the world, expands the reach of products and services of the company/institution. They can understand the growth in the market, demand in the market and competitors in the market. They may enhance the quality and control in the market too.

5. Reach to Unreached: There are several reasons to have a website, but this is the most appropriate reason to reach the unreached. Online marketing is one of the revolutions where selling and purchase is been in fashion now to deliver products and services in the areas where it is very difficult to be present physically. Therefore, now you can see that a person sitting in any remote region of Ladakh may access information and services of his/her choice through a website.

6. Information Dissemination : Information exchange and dissemination are some of the best reasons for having a website. Communication is very important in understanding the requirement of information of students, users, customers, etc. During the Covid-19 pandemic, it was seen that the growth and updating of websites increased in a great number. Because everyone was engaged to reach their users/customers through their website. Therefore, websites are a magical instrument in connecting people.

CREATING SITE

Creating and designing a website is a work of expertise. One has to understand the programming/coding language and knowledge of computer science. A professional website needs knowledge of web designing tools. But the revolution in this field also occurred during the last decade. The readymade templates-based website creating tools are now been available to everyone. They are almost free and having a very user-friendly plateform to create your own website. Some (Carney, 2020) of are:

1. sites.google.com
2. Webs.com
3. Wix.com
4. Weebly.com
5. Worldpress.com
6. Webnode.com
7. Site123.com .... Etc.

There are several free site development tools are available by which anyone may be able to create a website of their interest area. Among all google site is the best one. It gives a very simple and user-friendly option to create and customize the website. The support of google makes it more powerful in this genre. There is no space problem on the google site. The Google Drive cloud space is available for your website whereas others sometimes asking for money after creating a website. The website under google site is available in the search engine of Google whereas it is not available in the free version of others.

There are very easy steps to create a website through google sites:

(a) First, open the site https://sites.google.com/new

(b) Sign-in through your Gmail account, if you are not login into your Google chrome account through your Gmail account.

(c) At the bottom right, you have to choose the 'Create New Site' option and mention the name of your website i.e. Your Library name – Madhu Limaye Library

(d) All formatting like font size, color, picture, URL, etc. may be modified.

(e) Readymade 'Themes' templates are available; they can be changed at any time.

(f) The contents in the form of pages may be added.

(g) The six layouts are available under google sites, anyone may be chosen as per requirement.

(h) After all, edit work, you can see the preview of your website. After satisfying with your changes, you can publish it.

(i) After publishing, you will get an option of adding the 'web address' of your website. i.e. I have used web address 'mllrmlnlu'. After publishing it, You will get the web address - https://sites.google.com/view/mllrmlnlu/home.

(j) After publishing the website, it is available for all.

UPDATE AND PERSONALIZE YOUR SITE

The free version of the website will give you *https://sites.google.com/view/mllrmlnlu/home.* From the web address, you can see that name of your library URL is with *sites.google.com.* But the website may be personalized and customized. While entering the web address at the time of publishing it, you have one more option i.e., 'Custom URL' or under setting this may also be chosen at any point of time.

A domain name for your personalized website has to be purchased by any domain name service provider like- Google Domains, GoDaddy.com, 123Reg, Register.it, Wix.com, etc. After getting a valid domain name for your website, Google will verify and then authenticate the same to you. If, Madhu Limaye Library would like to have *www.mllrmlnlu.ac.in* for its website. The domain name has to be purchased first and then verified by the Google sites and after the verification, the personalized web address will be *www.mllrmlnlu.ac.in.*

SHARE AND COLLABORATE ON SITES

The website also may be shared by some other person who can edit or update the website. If you are collaborating your website with your peer or someone, it is a wonderful feature. i.e. suppose in your library you have assigned events to update to one staff and online databases and resources update to another staff, it can be done seamlessly. This is good when you are working on some important project and you need to update information frequently in a collaborative manner.

CONCLUSION

Website is supposed to be the mirror of any organization and individuals also. The digital environment requires digital awareness and the availability of information on the digital platform. The websites are one of the very important tools which enable to highlights the features and capabilities of an institution or company. The websites are a powerful tool to communicate, collaborate, share, and exchange information at any time anywhere round the clock. It breaks the hesitant environment by asking and giving feedback on particular issues and areas. The free version of readymade template-based website creating tools empowers everyone to represent themselves in a more fashioned manner. There is no need for any coding or programming language in designing the website. Of course, to design a professional and most technical website, proficiency and competency in computer programming and coding languages are required. The availability of free website designing tools like Google Sites empowered individuals to create their websites rather than blogs. Therefore, Google sites like free template-based tools are very powerful tools which are empowering a common man to develop their website and present themselves among the globe without any barriers.

REFERENCES

Carney, L. (2020). 10 Best Free Website Builders 2020: The Definitive List. *Website Builder Expert*. https://www.websitebuilderexpert.com/website-builders/free/

CERN. (2020). *A short history of the Web | CERN*. Retrieved December 10, 2020, from https://home.cern/science/computing/birth-web/short-history-web

MonsterPost. (2020). What is Dynamic website? - MonsterPost What is Dynamic website?What is Dynami. *MonsterPost*. Retrieved December 12, 2020, from https://www.templatemonster.com/blog/what-is-dynamic-website/

Nix, E. (2020). *The World's First Web Site*. HISTORY. Retrieved December 11, 2020, from https://www.history.com/news/the-worlds-first-web-site

Parachute. (2020). *Top 10 Benefits of Having a Website*. Retrieved December 11, 2020, from https://www.parachute.net/insights/top-10-benefits-of-having-a-website

TechTerms. (2020). *Static Website Definition*. Retrieved December 12, 2020, from https://techterms.com/definition/staticwebsite

WPBeginner. (2019, February 20). *Beginner's Guide: What is a Domain Name and How Does it Work?* WPBeginner. https://www.wpbeginner.com/beginners-guide/beginners-guide-what-is-a-domain-name-and-how-do-domains-work/

10

Blogging

Art of Communication

A blog or a weblog is an online journal or informational and simple website, which is publically accessible displaying information in the reverse chronological order, with the latest posts appearing first, at the top. The focus of a blog is on prominently displaying individual blog articles (called blog posts) by displaying them on the homepage of the blog. Jorn Barger coined the term 'weblog' on 17 December 1997 (Wortham, 2007). Peter Merholz coined the short form, 'blog', in 1999 (Merholz, 1999). People started writing blogs to write diary-style entries, the first informal blog was Links.net, created by Justin Hall in 1994 to publish his writing (Harmanci, 2005). In 1999, Blogger.com, the most popular blogging website was launched, which was later acquired by Google in February 2003. The same year, Matt Mullenweg and Mike Little, released WordPress as a blogging platform in May 2003.

A Blog can be part of a larger website. One person or a group of people for communicating and spreading information, news, stories, and articles that are the most relevant at a given time can develop it. Features like frequent updates, informal language, and opportunities for readers to engage, comment, and have a conversation, have made blogs very popular. There are about 60 million blogs online and about a third of all websites are blogs (Skrba, 2020). For some people, blogging can be a leisure activity but most people create a blog to show their passion, creativity, and promotion of business. By creating a blog, bloggers can express themselves and share information with others.

ADVANTAGES OF BLOGGING

- It can be made freely accessible to the public by using platforms that are very free and easy to learn;
- Readymade templates, customizable themes, fonts, and background make the blog look very beautiful;
- Material posted on blogs is automatically archived;
- Extensive use of hyperlinks to reference material is possible in blogs, links to pertinent resources can easily be provided;
- No formal training is required for blogging, the author can personally create and edited
- Blogs enable a communication platform where readers can also comment on any of the posts and the owner can also reply to comments;
- The facility of 'Rich Site Summary' or 'Really Simple Syndication' can also be enabled to the blog to give information about new posts to the readers and followers;
- Blogging enables bloggers to "syndicate" their blogs i.e. republishing the original post to other blogs and third party websites;
- Users can use subscribe or followers to their favorite blogs;
- Blogging can be used to make money, through placing ads on their site;
- Working in collaboration is possible for some of the blogging sites.

BLOG vs. WEBPAGE

- A blog is dynamic in Nature and blog posts are represented Chronological, keeping the newest entry at the top of the page, while a webpage is static where content is organized in pages;
- Blogs are very easy to edit, very less technical knowledge is required so they updated regularly by the author/ creator or contributor himself;
- It is very easy to incorporate annotated bibliography of internet resources for the use of blog readers whereas it is not possible in a webpage;
- Content of the blog always appears on top of Search engines because they are more up-to-date than static websites;
- Blogs are Interactive, reader can comments, poll, etc, while this feature cannot be a part of a website.

BLOG BUILDING PLATFORMS

Today many Blog Building Platforms are available of which some are opensource, some are free, some are proprietary and some charge a meager amount for some special services.

WordPress (www.wordpress.org) : It is a very popular platform for Self-Hosted Blogs. One has to have web hosting and a domain name for creating a blog using this platform.

Wix (www.wix.com) : Wix is an excellent drag-and-drop blog builder to create small websites. Wix is a subscription-based platform for building a blog and it offers different packages.

Weebly (www.weebly.com) : Weebly is a very popular platform that allows anybody to build their blogs quickly and with ease. It is a free website builder, and it's very easy to use;

Medium (www.medium.com) : Co-founder of Twitter, Ev Williams created Medium which has today over 60 million monthly active users. Creating a blog is free on Medium but its subscription is also there to access the upgraded features;

Ghost (www.ghost.org) : Ghost is a free and open-source blogging platform written in JavaScript and distributed under the MIT License. It works straight out of the box, requires no configuration, and is easy to master;

Tumblr (www.tumblr.com) : Tumblr is an American microblogging website founded by David Karp in 2007 and currently owned by Automatic. Tumblr's major differentiator is the free-form nature of the site and the ability of users to heavily customize their pages;

Joomla (www.joomla.org) : Joomla was launched in 2005 and has good user access controls and user management. It gives flexibility for displaying non-standard content types and has multilingual support built-in to the core and it even allows the use of different templates for different pieces of content;

Jimdo (www.jimdo.com) : Jimdo is a German website-builder and very popular site for Blogging. Jimdo offers few user-friendly elements that make it easy to manage and make changes in the blog. The basic version is free but the upgraded version provides built-in SEO tools for search engines and Customizable layouts, fonts, and colors;

Squarespace : Squarespace is the all-in-one platform to create a blog. It is available for a free 14-day trial. No Plugins are required to use and the drag and drop option makes it easy to use;

Blogger (www.blogger.com) : Blogger is a hosted blogging platform; the blog created by the user is hosted on the server of the blogger. It is a free platform but one may pay a meager amount to get the custom domain name. It is secure, reliable, and very easy to use.

The success of a blog somewhere also depends on the hosting site chosen for its creation. It is always advisable to choose the right tool after analyzing the range of the platform.

BLOGGER

Blogger is a blog-publishing service that allows multi-user blogs with time-stamped entries. It is a free but simplest blogging platform launched in 1999 by Pyra Labs which was later acquired by Google in 2003. It is a hosted blog platform so no hosting website is required and a person having a Google account can create a blog after following simple guidelines. No technical knowledge or coding experience is required to create a blog using blogger.com as it is quite intuitive in design and setup.

ADVANTAGES OF USING BLOGGER.COM TO CREATE A BLOG

- It is a very secure and reliable site and it is backed by Google;
- It is free anyone with a Gmail account can create a blog using subdomain via blogspot.com, provision of the customized domain is also available on meager payment;
- It is a very simple and user-friendly platform, no codding and technical knowledge is required to make a blog on blogger;
- All the features of the plugin are free and included inside itself only;
- Several templates are available, layout, background are customizable;
- There is no limit to creating any number of blogs with one Gmail account and there is no limit on the number of visitors;
- One can monetize the blog by integrating it with Google AdSense;
- Blog analytics is also integrated within the Blog settings

to assess the blog's traffic and see the content getting the most visits;

STEPS TO CREATE A BLOG USING BLOGGER.COM

- Plan about your blog (Content, target audience, pages, layout)
- Pick a blog name (Choose something descriptive).
- Get your blog online (Register your blog and get hosting).
- Customize your blog (Choose a free template and tweak it).
- Design your pages
- Write & publish your first post (The fun part!).
- Promote your blog (Get more people to read your blog).

STEPS TO CREATE A BLOG THROUGH BLOGGER

Create a blog through blogger is very simple. No professional or technical skill is required.

Sign in to Blogger : The first step is to sign in the blogger.com. One needs to have a Google account to access the dashboard of Blogger, so sign up for an account. If you already have it then skip this step and directly go to www.blogger.com, enter your 'Google Email' and 'password' into the 'Sign In' box on the right side of the screen and click Sign In. On signing, it will directly take you to create a new blog (Figure 1), name the blog, and click on next. It will ask for the URL of your blog. Write the preferred URL, Google will automatically check the availability, and in the next window enter your display name (displayed to readers of your blog and click on Finish. However, if you do not want to create the blog at that moment of time click on skip the first step, just write your display name, and click on finish. The soon you click on the finish you will enter the Blogger dashboard.

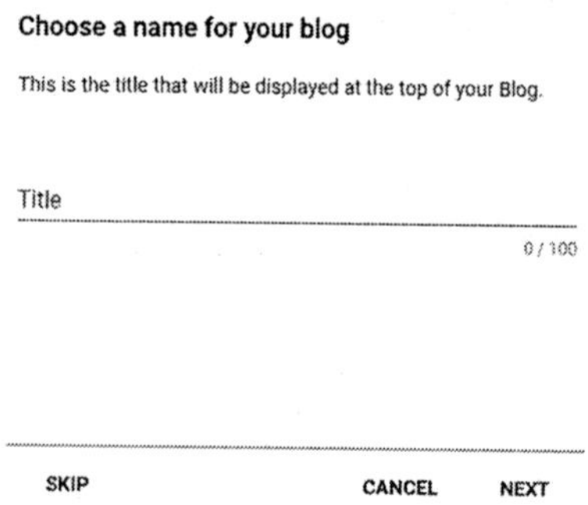

If you have created your blog in the first step name of your blog will be in the left upper corner of the dashboard otherwise click on the create a blog, name the blog, and URL of your blog, the blog will be created. In this way, your blog will be created, once you have created a blog you can change the theme, layout, other settings and create posts for your readers and viewers. You create as many as a blog by clicking the drop-down arrow near the name of your blog and selecting the new log from the options.

BASIC TABS

New Post : This helps to create a new post on the blog. A post or a blog post is an entry (article) that you write on a blog to publish insights, thoughts, and stories on any topic. A blog post will have a title and a body, which can include content in the form of text, photos, infographics, or videos. These blog posts are displayed chronologically on the blog with the newest on the top. One can do settings for how many posts should be displayed on the main page of the blog.

Posts : This tab tells about the number of posts on the blog. It displays the list of posts along with the date on which they are published; shortcuts to revert to draft, apply labels to this post, delete, view, number of comments on the post. It also has information about which collaborator created that post if the blog has more than one collaborator.

Stats : Stats tells about the overall statistics of a blog, number of followers, number of posts, and comments on the blog posts for a particular blog. Graphical representation of the views of the latest post (last 24 hours, last seven days, last 30 days, last 3/6/12 months or overall); overall blog, all posts, and all pages are included in the stats tab.

Comments : Comments displays all the comments on the blog chronologically irrespective of the posts on which it appeared, it has the name of the commenter, name of the post, comment, and date on which it is made. We can remove the content of any of the comments, or mark it as spam or permanently delete it from the blog.

Earnings : A blogger can earn money from ads by creating an AdSense account. Google AdSense is the most popular advertising program, launched by Google in mid-2003. It provides a good opportunity for website owners to monetize their traffic. Once a blogger creates accounts in AdSense, Google automatically places ads on the blog or website. The blogger gets revenue either on a per-click or per-impression basis.

Pages : Pages are the articles posted independently, which contain information about a specific topic. They are static. They are not part of the blog's timeline, rather they are linked from the main timeline and often include content like "Contact" or "About" or any other information that blogger want to share with his readers but don't expect to update frequently. They can be displayed as separate tabs on the top of the blog or the side of the blog. By default, the home page of a blog is the blogpost page, which displays the new posts published on the blog. A 'Page' usually has a 'Page Title', 'Page Content', and the comment section.

Layout : Layout is the most important menu of the blog, it helps in customization of the blog. A blogger can decide about the content on Navbar, Header, Cross Column, Sidebars, and Header & Footer of a blog. Through this menu, one can add remove and add gadgets in the blog. Blogger uses the term gadgets for widgets, which are a handy, easy, and simple way to add some flare to the blog.

Theme : Theme is there for customization of the blog by choosing the template and doing the other setting. A blogger can choose a theme by the information to be displayed on the blog, for example, a theme like 'Contempo' is best suited to adventurous blog as focus on photos and story, while the theme 'Soho' can be used for a blog which displays more of photos, designs or musings. Theme 'Emporio' can take an array of posts and display them in a neat and tidy way, while theme 'Notable' is like a notepad for scribbles, stories, and so much more. Other themes like 'Simple', 'Dynamic Views', 'Essential', 'Picture Window', 'Awesome Inc.', 'Watermark', 'Ethereal', 'Travel', etc are also available.

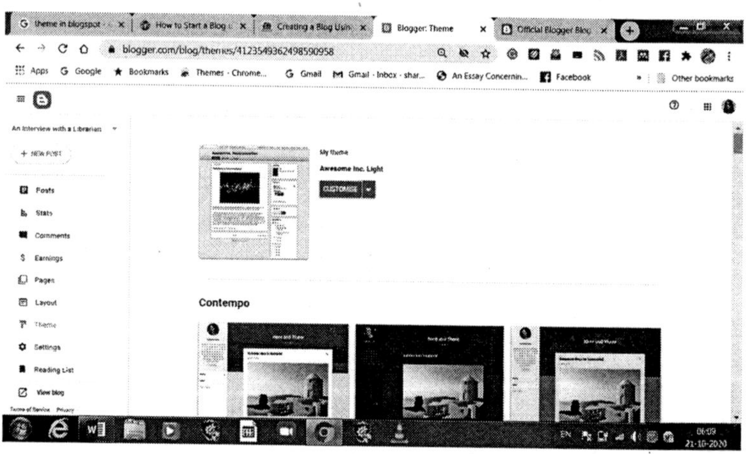

After choosing the appropriate theme, the blog can be customized also. Background of the blog can be changed, Widths of the blog and sidebars can be adjusted, body layout and the footer layout can be chosen and settings about font and text colour can be done.

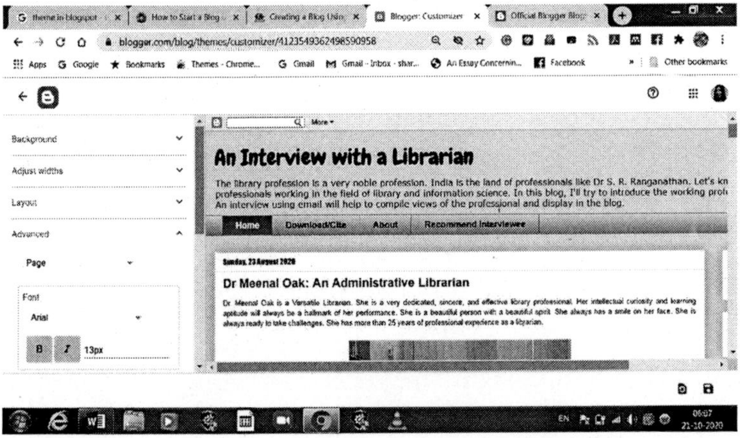

SETTINGS

Basic : Here you can do basic settings of the blog, which include Title, Description of the blog, Blog language, whether blog contains Adult content, and Google Analytics property ID. Here the author can also do the Privacy settings that blog is visible to search engine to find the blog, change the Blog Address or customize the domain, HTTPS redirect (Ensure that visits to HTTP redirect to HTTPS), set the Permissions to edit the blog, Add Blog Authors and decide about the reader's access.

Posts : Here it can be decided how many posts should be shown on the main page, decide about Archiving Frequency, decide about Post template (optional - preformat the post editor of each new post), Image lightbox to Showcase images in an overlay on top of post and Ideas panel to Show suggested topics and questions

Comments : Here decision about comment location (whether it should be embedded on the main page or it should appear as a full page or as a Popup window or it should be hidden), who can comment (users with Google Accounts or anyone or only members of the blog), Comment moderation, Reader comment captcha, Show word verification for readers who comment and Comment form message, are taken by the blogger.

Email : In this setting, the blogger has to decide on which email the notifications about the comments by the readers have to come.

Formatting : This setting section is for choosing the Time zone. Here setting can be done for date header format, archive index date format, timestamp format, and comment timestamp format. Settings about Search preferences (Meta tags and indexing terms), other (Import & back up, Delete Blog, Adult Content, Google Analytics), user settings (Profile of the blogger) can also be made here.

Other settings like enabling Meta tags and giving the search description; errors and redirects; crawlers and indexing; Monetisation; Manage blog (Import content, Back up content, Videos from the blog, Remove the blog); Site feed and General (Use Blogger draft and User profile) can be made from the last part of settings

Reading List : In the Reading List, we can add our favorite blogs.

View Blog : This will take us to our blog.

CREATE, EDIT, OR DELETE PAGES

- In the left menu, click Pages.
- **Create a new page :** Click the New page. Enter a page title and other information and click Save, Preview, or Publish.
- **Edit a page :** Under the page, you want to edit, click Edit. Update your page and click Save, Preview, or Publish.
- **Delete a page :** Under the page, you want to remove, click Delete and then Ok.

CREATE, EDIT, MANAGE OR DELETE A POST

The 'Post' is the life of the blog. Bloggers should be very

careful while creating a post, as whenever a post is created readers are notified. To create a new post:

- Click New Post
- Type the title of the Post
- Type the text in the body of the post
- A blogger can choose the toolbar to customize the content in the body of the post, settings about text font, size, colour, and alignment can be made. A text can be changed into a heading, subheading, or minor heading.

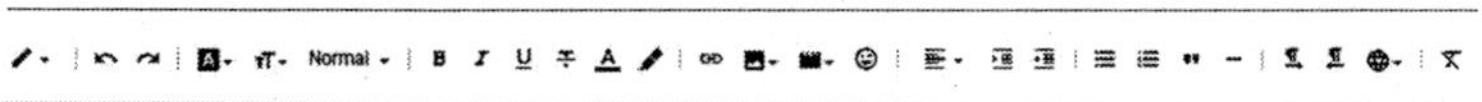

- Link to other websites, Images, Special Characters, Tables, Videos from devices, and YouTube videos can be added to the blog.
- To add a photo or video place the cursor where you want to add, now click on the icon of photo or video on the toolbar, a pop-up window will appear. A blogger can choose a photo from the blog library, or Google photos, or upload it for a device, once the content is uploaded, choose and Click to select, the content will be added to the body of the blog. The size of the photo and video can be adjusted to small, medium, large, extra-large or it can be kept in its original size. Alignment can also be done. In the same way, video can be uploaded from the device in the blog.
- Once you are finished with content posting you can check how your post will look when it is published, click Preview.
- You can also save it for the future or publish it, you can edit the posts, which have been already published, and you can even revert it to draft.
- You can also delete a post anytime you want.

WHAT CAN BE ADDED TO A POST

- Link to other websites
- Images
- Videos
- Special Characters.

ADDING GADGETS TO A BLOG

Gadgets are the tools or content that one can add, arrange or remove from the sidebar(s) of the blog; rather these are the blocks that make up the sidebars of a blog. At present provision of 26 gadgets is there in the blogger.com, which include:

- AdSense to earn revenue by displaying relevant ads on the blog.
- Featured post to highlight a special post on the blog.
- Blog search to let visitors search the blog.
- HTML/JavaScript to add third-party functionality or other code to the blog.
- Profile to display information about Blogger to the blog visitors.
- Blog Archive to help the visitors to navigate the blog with links to older posts.
- Page Header to display the blog's title and description.
- Followers to display a list of users who follow the blog.
- Image to add an image to the blog.
- Labels to show all the labels of posts in the blog.
- Pages to display a list of stand-alone pages on the blog.
- Link List to display a collection of various sites, blogs, or web pages for the visitors to get additional information.
- Text to add a text message to the blog.
- Popular Posts to display a list of the most popular posts from the blog.

- Blog's stats to display the number of page views to the blog.
- Blog List to display the list of other blogs.
- Follow by Email helps the visitors to subscribe to email delivery when you publish a new post on the blog.
- Feed helps to add content from an RSS or Atom feed to the blog.
- Logo to add a logo to the page.
- Subscription Links helps the readers of the blog to subscribe to the blog easily with popular feed readers.
- Translate helps the visitors to translate the blog into different languages.
- The list can be used to display a list to give extra information to the blog readers, which may include a list of your favorite books, films, or anything you like.
- Contact Form is used to add a contact form to the blog through which blog readers may send any query or ask for any information.
- Wikipedia can be used to create a search box to directly search on Wikipedia for articles or full text.
- Attribution is used to display the blog's attribution data.
- Report Abuse can be used by the reader of the blog to send a report to Google if he feels that some inappropriate content is available on the blog.

CONTENT TO AVOID

- Material hosted by someone else without their consent.
- Copyrighted materials.
- Content that violates the content policy. This includes, but is not limited to, explicit imagery posted without the subject's consent and hateful, violent, or crude content.

BLOGGING IN LIBRARIES

Blogging through Google Blogger is very easy. It is the most convenient free tool to design a blog. Libraries usually have a small attention on the institutions' website. By creating their blog, libraries can highlight their collection, services, and infrastructure to the readers. It is an efficient tool for marketing library events and resources. They can use blogs for disseminating professional and general information to their readers. Library professionals can manage the blog themselves, and they can reach their readers more frequently and efficiently.

REFERENCES

Fichter, D. (2003). Why and how to use blogs to promote library services. Marketing Library Services, 17(6). http://www.infotoday.com/mls/nov03/fichter.shtml

Harmanci, R. (2005-02-20). Time to get a life — pioneer blogger Justin Hall bows out at 31". San Francisco Chronicle.http://www.sfgate.com/cgi-bin/article.cgi?file=/c/a/2005/02/20/MNGBKBEJO01.DTL

Merholz, P. (1999). Peterme.com. Internet Archive. Archived from the original on, 10-13.https://web.archive.org/web/19991013021124/http://peterme.com/index.html

Schwartz, G. (2005). Blogs for libraries. WebJunction. http://webjunction.org/do/DisplayContent?id=767

Skrba, A. (2020) Blogging Statistics 2020: How Many Blogs Are Out There?https://firstsiteguide.com/blogging-stats/

Wortham, J. (2007). After 10 Years of Blogs, the future's brighter than ever. Wired. https://www.wired.com/entertainment/theweb/news/2007/12/blog_anniversary